# CHOCOLATE WAR

Start a New Cooking Chapter With Chocolate Dessert Cookbook

(A Yummy Chocolate Cookbook for Your Gathering)

**Pamela Wilson**

Published by Alex Howard

## © Pamela Wilson

All Rights Reserved

*Chocolate War: Start a New Cooking Chapter With Chocolate Dessert Cookbook (A Yummy Chocolate Cookbook for Your Gathering)*

**ISBN 978-1-990169-15-1**

All rights reserved. No part of this guide may be reproduced in any form without permission in writing from the publisher except in the case of brief quotations embodied in critical articles or reviews.

**Legal & Disclaimer**

The information contained in this book is not designed to replace or take the place of any form of medicine or professional medical advice. The information in this book has been provided for educational and entertainment purposes only.

The information contained in this book has been compiled from sources deemed reliable, and it is accurate to the best of the Author's knowledge; however, the Author cannot guarantee its accuracy and validity and cannot be held liable for any errors or omissions. Changes are periodically made to this book. You must consult your doctor or get professional medical advice before using any of the suggested remedies, techniques, or information in this book.

# Table of contents

**PART 1** ............................................................................................. 1

CHOCOLATE CREAM CAKE ............................................................... 2
CITRUS COCONUT CAKES ................................................................. 3
WHITE CHOCOLATE TRUFFLES .......................................................... 5
CHOCOLATE CARAMEL TARTS .......................................................... 6
DOUBLE-STRAWBERRY SAUCE WITH ICE CREAM ............................. 7
CHOCOLATE FUDGE SUNDAY ........................................................... 8
STRAWBERRY MERINGUES ............................................................... 9
CHOC-MINT ICE CREAM ................................................................. 10
ALMOND CAKE WITH APRICOT AND VANILLA BEAN SYRUP ........... 11
COCONUT CHOCOLATE CHIP COOKIES ........................................... 12
RASPBERRY CRÈME BRULEE ........................................................... 14
MINI EGGNOG CUPCAKES .............................................................. 16
CHART HOUSE MUD PIE ................................................................ 18
CHOCOLATE PAVLOVA ................................................................... 20
WATERMELON BARS ..................................................................... 22
CHOCOLATE PEANUT BUTTER TORTE ............................................. 27
BROWNIE CHEESECAKE BITES ........................................................ 30
CHOCOLATE MOUSSE .................................................................... 32
GLUTEN-FREE HUMMINGBIRD CAKE ............................................. 34
WHITE CHOCOLATE RASPBERRY BARS ........................................... 36
COFFEE PANNA COTTA .................................................................. 38
CHERRY LEMONADE DOUGHNUTS ................................................ 40
GOLDEN MOLASSES APPLE CAKE ................................................... 42
RED VELVET CAKELETTES ............................................................... 44
FROZEN CHOCOLATE CAPPUCCINO CRUNCH CAKE ........................ 46
BAKED APPLES WITH RAISINS ........................................................ 48
RAW VEGAN SNICKERS BARS ......................................................... 50
WHITE CHOCOLATE-GINGER MILK RICE WITH LIME AND BLUEBERRIES .......................... 52
FRUIT WHOLE WHEAT CRUMBLE ................................................... 54
CHERRY CHOCOLATE BAKED FAUXLASKA ...................................... 55
COCOA-GRAHAM SNACKWICHES .................................................. 56
CHOCOLATE-BANANA FREEZE ....................................................... 57

| | |
|---|---|
| Chocolate Crunchies | 58 |
| Chocolate Dipped Potato Chips | 59 |
| Chocolate Pudding Pie | 60 |
| Chocolate Silk Whip | 61 |
| Chocolate Toffee Chunks | 62 |
| Chocolate Whipped Cream | 63 |
| Chunky Chocolate Bark | 64 |
| Cinnamon-Spiced Hot Cocoa | 65 |
| Cocoa- Amaretto Crepes | 66 |
| Cocoa Rice Pudding | 68 |
| Cocoanut Candies | 69 |
| Flourless Chocolate Torte | 70 |
| Fudgy Brownies | 71 |
| Grilled Chocowich | 72 |
| Hot Fudge Sauce | 73 |
| Indoor S'mores | 74 |
| Miracle Mousse | 75 |
| Mud Pie | 76 |
| Mug O' Chocolate Cake | 77 |
| No-Bake Chocolate Wafer Cake | 78 |
| Peanutty Chocolate Pizza | 79 |
| Pepperminty Brownies | 80 |

## PART 2 ............................................................................................ 81

| | |
|---|---|
| 3d Chocolate Cheesecake | 82 |
| Apricot Cheesecake Tarts | 84 |
| Bittersweet Chocolate Cheesecake | 86 |
| Black Forest Cheesecake | 88 |
| Black Forest Cheesecakes | 91 |
| Blissful Peanut Butter-Chocolate Cheesecake | 93 |
| Blossom Cheesecake | 96 |
| Brownie Cheesecake | 99 |
| Brownie Swirl Cheesecake | 101 |
| Butterfinger Cheesecake | 103 |
| Candy Bar Cheesecake | 105 |
| Candy Cane Cheesecake | 107 |

| | |
|---|---|
| Cannoli Cheesecake | 109 |
| Cappuccino Cheesecake Pie | 111 |
| Caramel Chocolate Cheesecake Bites | 113 |
| Caramel Fudge Cheesecake | 115 |
| Caramel Stripe Cheesecake | 117 |
| Chilled Raspberry Cheesecake | 119 |
| Chocolate & Peanut Butter Mousse Cheesecake | 121 |
| Chocolate Almond Cheesecake | 123 |
| Chocolate Banana Cheesecake | 125 |
| Chocolate Berry Cheesecake | 127 |
| Chocolate Caramel Cheesecake | 129 |
| Chocolate Cheese Pie | 131 |
| Chocolate Cheesecake | 133 |
| Chocolate Cheesecake Bars | 136 |
| Chocolate Cheesecake Phyllo Tartlets | 138 |
| Chocolate Cheesecake Squares | 139 |
| Chocolate Cheesecake Triangles | 141 |
| Chocolate Cheesecakes | 143 |
| Chocolate Cherry Cheesecake | 145 |
| Chocolate Chip Cheesecake | 147 |
| Chocolate Chip Cheesecake Dessert | 149 |
| Chocolate Chip Cherry Cheesecake | 151 |
| Chocolate Chip Cookie Cheesecake | 153 |
| Chocolate Chip Cookie Dough Cheesecake | 155 |
| **CHOCOLATE CHIP COOKIE TART** | **158** |
| Chocolate Cookie Cheesecake | 160 |
| Chocolate Cran-Raspberry Cheesecake Bars | 162 |
| Chocolate Cranberry Cheesecake | 164 |
| Chocolate Glazed Cheesecake | 166 |
| Chocolate Macadamia Cheesecake | 169 |
| Chocolate Malt Cheesecake | 171 |
| Chocolate Mousse Cheesecake | 173 |
| Chocolate Peanut Butter Cheesecake | 175 |
| Chocolate Pecan Cheesecake | 178 |
| Chocolate Raspberry Cheesecake | 180 |

Chocolate Sandwich Cookie Cheesecake ....................................................... 182
Chocolate Swirl Cheesecake ..................................................................... 184
Chocolate Swirled Cheesecake .................................................................. 186

# Part 1

# Chocolate Cream Cake

A simple, 4-ingredient cake recipe that is perfect for afternoon tea.

You will need:

1/3 cup of chocolate drink
250 grams of Arnott's Choc Ripple Biscuits
600ml of thickened cream
Curls of white chocolate for topping

Procedure:

Beat chocolate drink and cream together with an electric mixer until it forms stiff peaks.

Spread some cream mixture on a plate for the base. Assemble biscuits on top of the other, sandwiching cream in between layers until it you create a "log". Make sure to leave some cream to coat the top and sides. Wrap and put in the fridge overnight.

Before serving, top the cake with curled white chocolate. Slice cake at an angle for full effect.

# Citrus Coconut Cakes

Not only will this dessert be an excellent chaser to an amazing dinner, but also diabetics and those who watch their sugar intake are welcome to enjoy it.
You will need:

1 tablespoon of desiccated coconut
¾ cup of self-rising flour
¼ cup of Equal Spoonfuls sweetener
1 Tablespoon of fine grated lemon rind
1 Tablespoon of fine grated orange rind
½ cup of skim milk
1 egg white lightly whisked
1 Tablespoon of melted butter
some more butter to grease the pan
Procedures:

Set and preheat your oven to 180°C. Lightly grease 12 round-bottom patty pans with the melted butter. Cook coconuts in a small non-stick frying pan until slightly toasted, making sure to keep stirring while doing so. Place coconuts in a small bowl and set aside.

In a mixing bowl, sift Flour and Equal Spoonfuls. Mix in the lemon and orange rinds until combines and create a well in the center. On a separate container, whisk the egg white, butter and milk then add to the flour.

Divide the mixture evenly on the 12 pans and sprinkle the coconut on top. Bake for 15 minutes or until poking the middle with a skewer comes out clean.

Let cakes cool on a rack for a couple of minutes and serve warm.

# White Chocolate Truffles

This simple to prepare yet elegant tasting dessert is great with coffee at any time of the day...or night.

You will need:

500 grams of white chocolate broken to pieces
180 grams of chopped plain, unsalted butter
2 tablespoons of vanilla extract
2 tablespoons of silver cachous

Procedures:

Place baking paper on a 2cmx8cm bar pan.

On a separate bowl, stir in the chocolate, butter and 2 tablespoons of warm water over low heat. Once it smoothens out, remove from heat and mix in your vanilla extract.

Pour the mixture on the bar pan and sprinkle the silver cachous on top. Refrigerate for 3 hours or until the mixture is set.

Cut into cubes and serve.

# Chocolate Caramel Tarts

This is an easy, no bake dessert that even kids will enjoy making. You will need:

Half a cup of Top 'n Fill filling
6cmx3cm high quality tart shells
100 grams of dark chocolate and some extra shavings for garnish
¼ cup of thin pure cream
Procedures:

Spread the caramel onto tart shells and chill. Melt the chocolate in a bowl on top of simmering hot water. Be careful not to let the bowl touch the water. When the chocolate is nice and smooth, spread chocolate over the tarts and chill again until set. Garnish with shaved chocolate before serving.

# Double-Strawberry Sauce With Ice Cream

This recipe will surely be a hit for strawberry and ice cream lovers whatever the occasion.

You will need:

Vanilla ice cream
250 grams of hulled strawberries plus an extra 125 grams hulled and cut into quarters
½ a cup of caster sugar
1 cup of dried strawberries

Procedures:

Over medium low heat, stir in the fresh strawberries, sugar and a cup of water until sugar is dissolved. Turn up the heat and bring to a boil. Lower the heat and let it simmer without stirring for 10 minutes, or until the strawberries soften.

Blend mixture with a stick blender until it becomes smooth. Add dried strawberries and cook over low heat for 5 minutes or until strawberries soften slightly. Set aside and let cool for 10 minutes. Stir in extra strawberries. Top on vanilla ice cream and serve.

# Chocolate Fudge Sunday

A good old classic that never gets old.
You will need:

100 grams of top quality dark chocolate (cooking chocolate) cut into squares
400 gram can of condensed skim milk (sweetened)
8 chocolate wafer biscuits
12 scoops of light and creamy vanilla ice cream
Procedures:

Cook condensed milk and chocolate over low heat while stirring using a metal spoon. Remove from pan and set aside after chocolate completely melts.

Layer ice cream, fudge alternately, and serve with the wafers.

# Strawberry Meringues

A delicious dessert that only takes less than five minutes to prepare.

You will need:

200 gram box of yoghurt (Greek-style)
4 meringue nests
A tablespoon of honey
250 grams washed Punnet Strawberries (hulled and cut in half)
30 grams crumbled Cadbury Flake bar
Procedures:

Mix honey and yoghurt in a mixing bowl. Top meringues with mixture, decorate with strawberries and crumbled flakes. Serve

# Choc-Mint Ice Cream

Chocolate and mint has always been meant for each other as seen in this dessert classic.
You will need:

2 teaspoons of Peppermint essence
½ a cup of thickened cream
2 liters of Choc-chip ice cream (softened)
some green food color
200 grams chopped Mint Slice biscuits
Procedure:

Mix the peppermint, cream, and tint with the food color. Combine with the softened ice cream adding biscuits in the mixture. Smoothen the surface and cover with cling wrap to prevent ice crystals to form. Freeze overnight.

# Almond Cake With Apricot And Vanilla Bean Syrup

Seasonal Apricots always make great desserts like this simple to do recipe that your family and guests alike will surely enjoy.

You will need:

250 grams of softened butter
2 cups of ground Almonds
4 eggs
¼ cup of rice flour
2/3 cup of caster sugar
Double cream for serving

*for the Apricot and Vanilla bean syrup

½ cup of caster sugar
1 Vanilla bean (split)
4 Apricots de-stoned and cut into thick wedges

Procedure:

Preheat the oven to 160°Celsius. Grease a 6cm deep, 22cm round cake pan and line the base and sides with wax paper.

Mix sugar and butter until they become light and fluffy. Add the eggs 1 by one, beating the mixture thoroughly after each egg. Add your flour and ground almonds to the mix. Put the mixture in the pan and bake for an hour and 15 minutes, or until a skewer comes out clean when poked in the center. Take it out the oven and let it cool for 10 minutes. Transfer the cake on to a wire rack and let it cool further for another 10 minutes.

With a sharp knife, scrape the seeds off the Vanilla bean.

# Coconut Chocolate Chip Cookies

This is a fun variation of everybody's favorite cookie: the chocolate chip cookie with a coconut twist! This recipe makes about 3 dozen.

Ingredients:

1 2/3 cups all-purpose flour

¾ cup of unsalted butter (let it soften at room temperature)

½ cup of brown sugar

½ cup of granulated sugar

1 tablespoon of vegetable shortening (let it soften at room temperature)

1 teaspoon of vanilla extract

¼ teaspoon of salt

½ teaspoon of baking soda

1 egg

1 cup of semi-sweet chocolate chips

1 ½ cups of shredded coconut (sweetened)

Steps:

Put the oven racks at very bottom and very top part of the oven. Preheat oven to 375° Fahrenheit. Using parchment paper, line some baking sheets and then set them aside.

Using a standing mixer that has a paddle attachment, cream the butter, shortening, the two types of sugar, vanilla, and the egg. Mix them together until thoroughly combined.

In small bowl, mix baking soda, baking powder, and flour. Add the butter mixture and mix until all are combined thoroughly.

Add the chocolate chips and the coconut until evenly distributed.

Using an ice cream scoop (the small one – about 1 tablespoon in measurement), scoop some cookie dough onto the baking sheets. Don't forget to put them a few inches away from each other.

Bake these for about 9-11 minutes, or till you see the edges become light golden in color. Allow them to cool completely.

You can store these in jars, in the refrigerator, or serve with vanilla ice cream to make a sandwich.

# Raspberry Crème Brulee

This is an interesting variation of the standard crème brulee. The tartiness of the raspberries makes the dessert much more delightful.

Ingredients:

½ cup lightly whipped heavy cream

1/3 cup confectioner's sugar

½ cup softened cream cheese (room temperature)

6-ounce container raspberries (fresh)

2 tablespoons granulated sugar (add extra for sprinkling purposes)

1 tablespoon lemon juice

1 teaspoon lemon zest

2 teaspoons vanilla extract

Steps:

In a saucepan (small), place the berries, 1 tablespoon of lemon juice, and 2 tablespoons of sugar. Heat the mixture until the berries begin to burst. Turn off the heat.

In a clean bowl, mix the cream cheese, vanilla extract, lemon zest, and confectioner's sugar until everything becomes creamy.

Fold into the mixture the whipped cream. Set it aside for a while.

Divide evenly the berry mixture into 4 ramekins (6-ounce). You should then divide the mixture you set aside (cream) evenly into 4. Place the cream mixture on top of the berries in the ramekins. Be sure that the top is smooth before moving on.

Sprinkle approximately about a tablespoon of sugar on the top of the cream mixture in each ramekin. Using a blow torch, you could then caramelize the sugar on top. Make sure that the sugar becomes golden brown in color and is bubbly. If you do not have a blow torch, you can pop the ramekins under a broiler.

Let the crème brulee cool for 5 minutes or so before serving them.

# Mini Eggnog Cupcakes

Everybody will surely love these cupcakes as they are made from eggnog! This recipe makes about 32 cupcakes.

Ingredients:

For the batter (cake)

1 ¼ cups of cake flour

1 teaspoon of baking powder

¼ teaspoon of salt

½ teaspoon baking soda

1 teaspoon nutmeg

¼ cup unsalted butter (should be at room temperature)

¼ cup vegetable oil

1 cup of granulated sugar

1/3 cup eggnog

1 teaspoon vanilla extract

2 eggs

For the frosting

4 ounces cream cheese that has been softened (room temperature)

2 cups confectioner's sugar

2 tablespoons unsalted butter, softened (room temperature)

½ teaspoon vanilla extract

¼ teaspoon nutmeg

2 tablespoons eggnog

Steps:

Preheat oven to 350°. Line some muffin tins (mini) with liners. Set them aside.

Whisk the first 5 ingredients for the cake batter in a small bowl.

Using a hand-held whisk, cream butter, sugar, and oil in a large bowl. Do this for about a minute or so, until the mixture becomes nice and fluffy.

Incorporate the eggs and vanilla. Continue to whisk until everything is pale in color and smooth. Add the eggnog and continue mixing.

Add in dry ingredients (from the small bowl) and mix everything. Continue mixing until the batter becomes nice and smooth.

Using an ice cream scoop (small), divide the batter into the muffin tins evenly. Bake them for 12-14 minutes or till the cupcakes have been cooked through fully. Allow the cupcakes to cool completely.

For the frosting, in a large bowl, add butter, cream cheese, and vanilla. Using a hand-held whisk, cream everything together.

Add the remaining ingredients and continue mixing until the frosting is nice and creamy.

When your cupcakes are cooled completely, fill a piping bag that has been fitted with a plain large tip with frosting. Decorate the cupcakes. You can then top them with sprinkles.

# Chart House Mud Pie

This is a fun dessert that ice cream lovers will surely love. It is very easy to make, and this could serve as the perfect comfort food, too.

Ingredients:

7-ounce package chocolate wafers, crushed

½ cup butter, softened

3 cups vanilla ice cream

3 cups chocolate ice cream

1 cup chocolate fudge sauce

Steps:

Mix butter and crushed wafers in a bowl. Be sure to mix both ingredients well.

In a 10-inch springform cake pan, spread the butter and crushed wafers mixture onto the bottom. Be sure to spread them out evenly.

For the ice cream, take them out of the freezer until they become pliable. Take note that the ice creams should simply be pliable, but not melting.

Using an electric mixer mix the ice creams. Mix the ice creams just enough to create a marbled effect. If you do not have an electric mixture, you can also mix the ice creams by hand, whichever works best for you.

Using a spatula, fill the cake pan with the ice cream mixture. Be sure to smooth the top when you are done.

Drizzle the top with the chocolate fudge sauce. You can decorate the top any way you want it.

Place the cake inside the freezer just until the chocolate hardens. When it hardens, cover the top of the cake pan with a sheet of waxed paper.

Finish freezing for 12 hours before serving.

Top with whipped cream if desired and serve.

# Chocolate Pavlova

This is an interesting chocolate dessert that will surely fascinate your guests. This recipe can serve 8.

Ingredients:

6 egg whites (large)

1 cup sugar

1 teaspoon balsamic or white wine vinegar

¼ cup cacao powder

1 teaspoon vanilla extract

¼ teaspoon salt

Berries and chocolate shavings for garnishing

For the cream:

1 ½ cups heavy cream

2 tablespoons powdered sugar

Steps:

Sift the cacao powder and then set aside.

Preheat the oven 300°. On a piece of parchment paper, using an 8-inch pie plate as your guide and a pencil, draw an 8-inch circle. Turn it over and place it on a baking sheet. Set these aside.

Using a standing mixer that has a whisk attachment, beat the salt and the egg whites until they become stiff peaks. Be careful that they do not dry out.

Before whisking, make sure that the bowl and the whisk are very clean, without any residue or else the egg whites will not whip.

As the beater continues to run, slowly add in a tablespoon of sugar at a time. Beat the mixture until everything becomes thick and glossy. Do not go overboard with the beating as the mixture will deflate.

With a spatula, fold in cocoa powder, vanilla, and vinegar. Be careful that the egg whites do not deflate.

Spoon the mixture into the center of the circle that you previously drew on the parchment. Using a spatula or a spoon, spread the mixture evenly to fit within the 8-inch circle. Make sure that you have a slight edge.

Bake this pavlova for an hour and 10 minutes. Once you are done, turn the oven off, open the door of the oven slightly, and let the pavlova cool inside the oven completely. Some even let the pavlova cool overnight.

In a big bowl, whisk the heavy cream. Do this until the cream creates soft peaks.

Add in the sugar and then continue to whisk until you create stiff peaks. Set this aside in the refrigerator until you are to use it already.

When you are ready, place the whipped cream on top of the pavlova. Spread it out until it covers the top of the pavlova. Scatter your berries on the top and garnish with chocolate shavings.

# Watermelon Bars

These bars are simply refreshing and wonderful. These are perfect after a heavy meal or simply as a snack.

Ingredients:

box of round vanilla wafers, ground finely

1 stick unsalted butter, melted

5 cups of watermelon juice (approximately about half of a large watermelon)

½ teaspoon lemon zest

½ cup lemon juice, fresh

½ cup sugar

½ cup heavy cream

4 small envelopes unflavored gelatin

¼ cup confectioner's sugar, or a cup of whipped cream

Instructions:

Preheat the oven to 350° Fahrenheit. Line a baking pan (13"x9") with foil. Be sure to leave a 2-inch overhang along the long sides of the pan. With cooking spray, spray the foil.

Mix the finely ground wafers with the melted butter. Add in 2 tablespoons water. Mix these well. To form a crust, press the crumb mixture onto the bottom of the pan that was previously prepared. Bake the crust for about 20 minutes and then let it cool.

In a small bowl, set aside the 2 cups of watermelon juice. In a large bowl, combine the lemon zest, sugar, heavy cream, lemon juice, and the remaining amount of watermelon juice.

In the small bowl with 2 cups of watermelon juice, sprinkle the gelatin. Let the mixture sit for 2 minutes, to let the gelatin dissolve and "bloom", or soak in liquid. When the gelatin has been left for 2 minutes, heat the mixture in the microwave for 2 minutes (high). You can also opt to heat the mixture in a small pot on the stove top. Check that the gelatin has completely melted and the mixture is smooth.

Mix the watermelon juice with the melted gelatin in the larger bowl. Stir the mixture to combine. Then, gently pour it onto the prepared crust and put the pan in the freezer for 2 hours or so, until the gelatin becomes firm. If using the refrigerator, the gelatin will set for 3-4 hours.

Be sure to keep the pan in the refrigerator until you are ready to serve. Before serving, cut it into squares. You can sprinkle the top with confectioner's sugar or whipped cream if desired.

# Gingerbread Tiramisu Trifle

This sweet treat will surely make a lot of people happy! This recipe serves 10-12.

Ingredients:
For the gingerbread:
2 1/3 cups flour
1 teaspoon baking soda
2 teaspoons ginger
1 teaspoon cinnamon
½ teaspoon cloves
½ teaspoon salt
1 cup molasses
1 cup sour cream
½ cup unsalted butter, room temperature
2 teaspoons lemon zest
¼ cup sugar
1 egg
½ teaspoon vanilla extract
For the filling (mascarpone)
1 ½ cups heavy cream

16 ounces softened Mascarpone cheese

1/3 cup granulated sugar

1 teaspoon vanilla extract

For the syrup

1 cup sugar

1 ginger tea bag

Steps:

Preheat the oven to 350°. Line with parchment paper a baking pan (9"x13") and then spray it with a nonstick spray. Set these aside.

Whisk flour, salt, baking soda, cinnamon, ginger, and cloves in a bowl and set aside.

Using a standing mixer that has a paddle attachment, cream the sugar, lemon zest, and butter. This will take about a minute or until the mixture becomes fluffy.

Mix in the eggs, vanilla, and the molasses for a minute. Add the sour cream and the dry ingredients. Mix everything just long enough for everything to be mixed well, but make sure that you do not overmix.

Pour the mixture onto the pan and then bake it for 25 minutes or until the cake is fully cooked.

Let the cake cool completely. When fully cooled, cut it into slices that are about ½" thick.

For the syrup, boil a cup of water then add the tea bag. Turn the heat off, and let the tea bag steep.

Take out the tea bag after a few minutes, then turn on the heat (medium) and mix in the sugar. Let the tea mixture cook around 5 minutes or until all of the sugar has dissolved. Let the syrup cool completely.

For the filling, in a standing mixer that has a whisk attachment, beat the heavy cream. Continue until you form stiff peaks. Pour the cream into a bowl and let it stay in the refrigerator for a few minutes.

Using the same bowl, cream the mascarpone, sugar, and vanilla. Do this for about 2 minutes, using medium speed.

Fold in the whipped cream using a spatula. After this, set the filling aside.

To assemble the trifle, get a trifle dish (14 cup measure or so) and cover the bottom with half a cup of the mascarpone filling. Take about a third of the cake slices and place them on the filling. Drizzle about a third of the syrup over the cake slices, and top them again with a third of the filling. Repeat the steps two more times.

Using plastic wrap, cover the trifle and put it in the refrigerator. Leave it there for 8 hours or overnight.

# Chocolate Peanut Butter Torte

This is a great torte to serve during special occasions or when you simply want to indulge your palate.

Ingredients:

Crust
- ☐ 32 Oreo cookies (crushed finely into crumbs)
- ☐ 5 1/3 tablespoons of unsalted butter (should be melted and completely cooled)
- ☐ A pinch of salt

Crunch
- ☐ ½ cup finely chopped salted peanuts
- ☐ ½ cup chocolate chips (mii)
- ☐ 2 teaspoons of sugar
- ☐ ½ teaspoon of espresso powder
- ☐ ¼ teaspoon of ground cinnamon
- ☐ Some ground nutmeg

Filling
- ☐ 2 cups of heavy cream
- ☐ 1.25 cups sifted confectioner's sugar
- ☐ 12 ounces of cream cheese, in room temperature
- ☐ 1 ½ cups peanut butter (creamy)
- ☐ 2 tablespoons of whole milk
- ☐ ¼ cup finely chopped salted peanuts

Topping
- ☐ 4 ounces finely chopped bittersweet chocolate
- ☐ Half cup heavy cream
- ☐ ½ cup finely chopped salted peanuts

Steps:
1) Preheat the oven to 350° Fahrenheit. Butter a springform pan (9-inch) and place it on a baking sheet.
2) Mix the melted butter, salt, and Oreo crumbs in a small bowl to form the crust. Toss the Oreo crumbs around using a fork to

make sure that everything is moistened. Pour the mixture onto the bottom of the pan and press down to form a thin layer.

3) Place the crust in the freezer for about 10 minutes. After that, bake it in the oven for another 10 minutes. Take the crust out after that time and transfer it on a wire rack and leave it to cool completely.

4) In another small bowl, mix mini chocolate chips, half cup of the peanuts, espresso powder, a dash of nutmeg, sugar, and cinnamon, to create the crunch. Toss all the ingredients using a fork and set aside.

5) For the filling, using a stand mixer that has a whisk, whip the 2 cups of cream until you see medium peaks. Add in a quarter of a cup confectioner's sugar and continue whipping until the peaks are medium-firm. Transfer the cream into another bowl and put in the refrigerator until it is ready to use.

6) Wipe the bowl of the stand mixer and replace the whisk attachment with the one with the paddle. Beat together the cream cheese plus the remaining cup confectioner's sugar. Continue to do this on medium speed till the cream cheese becomes smooth as satin. Add in the whole milk, peanut butter, and quarter of a cup of the chopped peanuts. Mix until fully combined.

7) To lighten the mousse, gently stir about a quarter of the whipped cream with a large rubber spatula. Add in the crunch mixture, then fold in the remaining cream.

8) Transfer the mousse onto the crust. Be sure to smooth out the top. Refrigerate the torte for 4 hours (This is the very least time it should be refrigerated. It would be best to do this overnight). Once the mousse becomes firm, cover it with plastic wrap.

9) To finish, a bowl that is heatproof should be placed over a saucepan that has simmering water. Place the chopped chocolate in the bowl and let it start to melt. When this happens (about 3 minutes), take the bowl out of the saucepan.

10) Make the half cup of cream boil and then pour it over the melted chocolate. Stir the mixture gently using a rubber spatula to form a ganache.

11) Transfer the ganache onto the top of the torte and smooth it out using a metal icing spatula. Spread the peanuts on top and let the torte chill. This will help to set the ganache. When the topping is already firm, take out the sides of the pan. Place the torte in the fridge until you are ready.

# Brownie Cheesecake Bites

This is a delightful mix of 2 favorite desserts: the brownie and the cheesecake. This recipe makes about 30 servings.

Ingredients:
- ¼ cup unsalted butter
- 2/3 up semisweet chocolate chips
- **2 eggs**
- 1/8 teaspoon salt
- ½ teaspoon vanilla extract
- 2/3 cup all-purpose flour
- 1 tablespoon cocoa powder
- 1 cup granulated sugar

Cheesecake filling
- 3 ounces cream cheese, left at room temperature
- 1 ½ tablespoons sugar
- 1 egg yolk, small

Steps:
1. Preheat the oven to 350°. Line a 30-piece mini muffin tin with liners. Set these aside.
2. Melt butter and chocolate in the microwave and then stir.
3. Beat sugar and eggs in a large bowl until the mixture becomes foamy and light. Add the chocolate mixture and vanilla. Stir until everything is well-combined.

4. Add in the cocoa, flour, and salt. Mix well. Be careful to mix only until all of the ingredients are fully combined.
5. Using a small ice cream scoop or spoon, fill in each of the lined muffin cup about 2/3 full.
6. For the cream cheese filling, cream the sugar, egg yok, and the cream cheese. Using a small spoon, place a little amount of the cream cheese mixture on the top of each brownie.
7. Let the mixture bake for 20 minutes in the oven. Let them cool completely before serving. An optional way to serve this is by dusting some confectioner's sugar on top for that extra sweetness.

# Chocolate Mousse

This is basically one of the staples when it comes to desserts. Even kids love chocolate mousse! This recipe serves 2.

Ingredients:

1/3 cup chopped bittersweet chocolate

1 tablespoon water

¼ teaspoon instant espresso powder

1 egg yolk

1 tablespoon unsalted butter

1 egg white

½ teaspoon vanilla extract

2 tablespoons granulated sugar

½ cup heavy cream

Steps:
1.   Whisk the heavy cream in a bowl until it has stiff peaks. Place this in the refrigerator until it is ready to be used.
2.   Whisk the sugar and egg yolk in a small bowl for 2-3 minutes or till the mixture becomes pale in color and thick. The sugar should also be dissolved. Set the mixture aside.
3.   In a saucepan (small), place about an inch of water and let it simmer. Put a small bowl over the saucepan and then add the

chocolate, espresso, butter, and water. This should be done over very low heat. Cook everything until the chocolate starts to melt.

4. Spoon in about a quarter of the chocolate into the egg mixture and mix it. Do this until the chocolate is combined. This is just to temper the eggs. You should then pour the egg mixture into the small bowl that is still in the simmering water. Stir the mixture constantly.

5. Add the vanilla extract and continue cooking over low heat until the mixture starts to thicken. Let the mixture cool but keep stirring frequently.

6. In another small bowl, whisk the egg white until it has stiff peaks. Once these appear, you can then fold in the egg white into the cooled chocolate mixture.

7. Fold the mixture into the whipped cream. Be careful not to overmix, or your heavy cream will lose the texture. Fold it in gently and only until everything is combined.

8. Put the mixture into cups and then refrigerate. It is best to leave it in the refrigerator for 4-6 hours.

# Gluten-Free Hummingbird Cake

This is for people who are looking for gluten-free desserts, or for those who simply want to try something new.

Ingredients:
- ☐ 3 cups of gluten-free flour
- ☐ 2 cups of white sugar
- ☐ **5 eggs**
- ☐ 1 cup pecans, chopped
- ☐ 1 ½ cups bananas, mashed
- ☐ 1 can (8 ounces) crushed pineapple with juice
- ☐ 1 teaspoon of ground cinnamon
- ☐ 1 ½ teaspoons of xanthan gum
- ☐ 1 teaspoon of salt
- ☐ 1 teaspoon of baking soda
- ☐ 1 ¼ cups of vegetable oil
- ☐ 1 ½ teaspoons of vanilla extract

For the icing
- ☐ ½ cup butter, chilled
- ☐ 3 8-ounce packages cream cheese, chilled
- ☐ 1 ½ cups confectioner's sugar

Steps:
1. Preheat the oven to 350° Fahrenheit. Mix together gluten-free flour, baking soda, xanthan gum, salt, ground cinnamon, and white sugar in a bowl. Set this aside.
2. In another bowl, beat the eggs until they become frothy. Add the beaten eggs into the flour mixture, as well as the oil. Be sure to mix everything well by hand. When everything has been mixed well, you can then add the chopped pecans.
3. After the pecans, you can then add into the mixture the bananas and the crushed pineapple with juice. Mix well. After that, add the vanilla extract and mix it, too. Do not be surprised if the batter is thicker than usual cake batters. Set this aside

4. Take the baking pan and flour it. Transfer the batter into the baking pan using a spatula. Smoothen it out so that the batter is flat.
5. Bake the cake for about 25-30 minutes or until it is fully cooked through. Let it cool for about 10 minutes and take it out from the oven.
6. For the icing, the ½ cup chilled butter should be beaten to make it soft. The chilled cream cheese should also be added to the butter and combined well.
7. After that, the vanilla should be added. After mixing the vanilla, 1 ½ cups of confectioner's sugar should be added slowly. This should be blended well until it becomes light and fluffy.
8. The icing should then be layered on and you can garnish it with additional pecans.

# White Chocolate Raspberry Bars

Raspberries are known for their tart flavor, making them refreshing additions to desserts. The berries plus the white chocolate will surely reel a lot of people in. This recipe makes around 18 bars.

Ingredients:

2 cups white chocolate chips

½ cup unsalted butter, at room temperature

1 cup flour (all-purpose)

2 eggs

0.5 cup granulated sugar

1 teaspoon vanilla extract

½ teaspoon salt

½ cup raspberry jam (seedless)

0.5 cup sliced almonds

Steps:
1. Preheat oven to 350°. Line a baking dish (9x9) using parchment paper. Spray it with non-stick cooking spray and set them aside.
2. Inside a microwaveable bowl, add a cup of white chocolate chips and butter. Melt these inside the microwave for a minute or till everything is fully melted and smooth.
3. In a big bowl, whisk the sugar and eggs together until everything is pale in color and light. Add the white chocolate mixture and gently whisk until everything is combined.
4. Add in salt and flour and mix again. Take your prepared pan and put 2/3 of the batter at the bottom. Bake this for about 15 minutes or till it becomes light golden brown in color.
5. In a saucepan (small), warm the jam till it becomes runny in consistency. Spread the jam onto the crust you just baked.

6. Add the remaining chocolate to the batter. Place spoonfuls of the mixture on the jam and sprinkle the almonds on top. Place this back in the oven for another 25 minutes or till the edges of the bars become brown.
7. Let this cool completely and then you can start cutting it into squares.

# Coffee Panna Cotta

This is a very tasty spoon dessert, and it is perfect for a hot afternoon. For coffee lovers out there, this is the perfect dessert!

Ingredients:
- ☐ 2 cups heavy cream
- ☐ 2/3 cup espresso coffee
- ☐ ½ cup sugar
- ☐ 8 grams gelatin sheets
- ☐ ½ vanilla pod

For the sauce
- ☐ 100 g chocolate (or 3 5ounce bars)
- ☐ 1/3 cup espresso coffee

Steps:
1. Soak the gelatin sheets in very cold water. The vanilla pod should be cut in half. The inner seeds should be scraped using the back of a knife.
2. In a saucepan, mix the coffee and heavy cream. Add in the sugar and the vanilla pod plus the seeds. Bring all of these almost to a boil.
3. Going back to the gelatin, check if the sheets have softened. If they have, squeeze out the excess water, and add them into the cream mixture. Let the gelatin melt for a few seconds and strain the mixture.

4. Divide the mixture into 6 moulds or around 125 ml each. Put the molds into the refrigerator for at least 4 hours to let them set.
5. For the sauce, melt the chocolate inside a bain marie. Once the chocolate has melted, add in the hot coffee. Stir the mixture until it becomes thick and creamy.
6. Take out the panna cotta from the moulds, garnish with coffee sauce and chocolate. You can top it all off with some coffee beans or chocolate.

# Cherry Lemonade Doughnuts

This is a fun and refreshing twist to the traditional doughnuts. This recipe makes about 5 dozen mini doughnuts.

Ingredients:

For the doughnuts
- ☐ ½ cup unsalted butter at room temperature
- ☐ 1 cup granulated sugar
- ☐ Lemon zest (1 lemon)
- ☐ **2 eggs**
- ☐ ½ cup cherry juice (or juice from ¾ cup of pitted cherries that have been blended and strained)
- ☐ 1 ½ cups flour
- ☐ 1 teaspoon baking powder
- ☐ 1 teaspoon salt

For the glaze
- ☐ 3 tablespoons lemon juice
- ☐ 3 tablespoons cherry juice (or juice from 5 pitted cherries that have been blended and strained)
- ☐ 2 cups powdered sugar

A quick tip: When blending cherries, it is very important to strain it and then add it to the batter or the glaze immediately. Setting it aside even for a few minutes will allow it to oxidize and turn into a brownish-purple liquid, which is not that great to look at.

Steps:
1. Preheat the oven to 400°. Place a rack at the center. Butter and flour the mini doughnut pans and put them aside.
2. Cream the sugar, lemon zest, and butter until the mixture becomes light and fluffy. Incorporate the eggs and then blend them well together. Mix in the half cup cherry juice.
3. In another bowl, whisk baking powder, salt, and flour together. Add in the cherry mixture until the color is smooth and uniform.

4. Using a large pastry bag that has a round tip, fill the bag with the batter. Pipe the batter carefully into the mini doughnut pans that have been prepared earlier. To make them perfect, each circle should only be filled about 2/3 to ¾ full.

5. Bake the doughnuts for 5 minutes or until the edges become light golden brown and the tops of the doughnuts are matte in color and springy when touched. Let the doughnuts cool for a few minutes in the pans and then flip them out on a cooling rack.

6. In a small bowl, whisk the cherry juice, lemon juice, and powdered sugar. Continue whisking until you have the desired consistency. When you stir the glaze, the glaze should have swirls on top, but they disappear slowly. If the swirls disappear immediately, this is a sign that you need more powdered sugar.

7. Dip the top of the doughnuts in the glaze and then give it a few taps. Place them on the rack to set.

# Golden Molasses Apple Cake

For apple lovers, this is a delightful cake to eat at any time of the day. The molasses gives extra flavor to this cake. This recipe serves 6 to 8.

Ingredients:

2 large eggs

2 large egg yolks

1 cup brown sugar

½ cup molasses

3 apples, cored, peeled, and diced into small cubes

1 tablespoon grated orange rind

1 ½ cups pastry flour

2 teaspoons baking soda

2 teaspoons baking powder

2 tablespoons cinnamon

A pinch of salt

Steps:
1. Preheat the oven to 300° Fahrenheit. Line the bottom of the springform cake pan (9 inches) with waxed paper shaped into a circle. Butter the paper plus the sides of the pan. Set this aside.
2. In a bowl, put all of the eggs. Add in the molasses and the brown sugar. Beat this for 3 minutes using an electric hand mixer until everything is well-combined.
3. Stir in the orange rind and the apples
4. Sift the baking soda, flour, baking powder, cinnamon, and salt all together. Re-sift everything into the cake batter while mixing the batter with a wooden spoon.

5. Transfer the batter into the prepared cake pan. Bake the cake for 60 to 65 minutes or until the cake is fully cooked through.
6. Let the cake cool in the pan slightly before taking it out of the mold. Finish the cooling on a wire rack.
7. You can serve the cake with whipped cream or some vanilla ice cream.

# Red Velvet Cakelettes

This is a perfect treat for those who love red velvet. This is also perfect for small gatherings or for children.

Ingredients:
- 2 ½ cups sifted cake flour
- 2 tablespoons of unsweetened cocoa powder
- 1 teaspoon of salt
- 1 ½ cups of sugar
- 1 ½ cups of vegetable oil
- 2 large eggs in room temperature
- ½ teaspoon of red food coloring (gel type)
- 1 cup of buttermilk
- 2 teaspoons of distilled white vinegar
- 1 teaspoon of pure vanilla extract
- 1 ½ teaspoon baking soda

For the cream cheese frosting
- 1 package or 8 ounce package softened cream cheese
- ¼ cup softened butter
- 1 teaspoon vanilla
- 1 package or 16 ounces powdered sugar, sifted

Steps:
1. Preheat the oven to 350° Fahrenheit. Whisk salt, cocoa, and flour together in a bowl.

2. Using an electric mixer set in medium-high, whisk in the sugar and oil till everything is well-combined. Add in the eggs, one by one. Beat the mixture until each egg is well-combined. If needed, scrape down the sides of the bowl so that everything is well-mixed. Mix in the food coloring and vanilla.

3. On low speed, incorporate the flour mixture in three different batches. Alternate with two additions of the buttermilk and whisk well after you add. Stir the vinegar and baking soda in a small bowl, and you will see it start to foam. Add this mixture to the batter and mix everything on medium speed for about 10 seconds.

4. Put butter and flour on a 13"x9" cake pan. Pour the batter into it. Bake the cake for 20 to 30 minutes, or until you do the toothpick test (insert a toothpick in various places of the cake and it comes out clean).

5. Put the cake on a wire rack to let it cool completely. Once completely cooled, put it in the freezer for approximately 15 minutes.

6. For the cake's frosting, beat the butter, cream cheese, and vanilla in a bowl using an electric mixer on medium speed. Add sugar slowly, beating until everything is well blended after you add the sugar.

7. Cut the cake into halves and fill with half of the frosting. The other half will then be used on the top of the cake. Decorate the cake as you desire and cut into small pieces.

# Frozen Chocolate Cappuccino Crunch Cake

This is ideal for chocolate and coffee lovers out there. The extra crunch also makes this a very special treat. The recipe is good for approximately 16 servings.

Ingredients:

1 frozen pound cake (10 ½ ounces), thawed

¾ cup heavy cream for whipping

11 ½ ounces chocolate chips (milk chocolate)

4 cups coffee-flavored ice cream, softened

1 cup of frozen prepared whipped topping, thawed

1 ¾ cups of malted milk balls, crushed coarsely

For topping:

Prepared whipped topping, thawed

Coarsely crushed malted milk balls

Steps:

1. Slice the cake into ¼" or 1/8" slices. Put half of the slices of cake on the bottom of a springform pan (9-inch). Be sure to press the cakes down firmly. Set aside the remaining slices.

2. In a medium saucepan, bring the cream to just a boil. Remove from the heat and add the milk chocolate. Let it stand for about 5 minutes.

3. After 5 minutes, mix or whisk the chocolate mixture until it becomes smooth.

4. Pour about half of the mixture over the pound cake inside the pan. Spread it evenly up to within ¼"inch edge of the pan. Cover this and freeze for approximately 1 ½ hours or till the chocolate has set.

5. Mix the ice cream plus the whipped topping inside a large bowl. Add in the 1 ¾ cups malted milk balls that have been crushed.

6. Spread this over the chocolate layer of the cake. Cover this again and freeze for at least another 6 hours.

7. To serve, take out the sides of the pan and garnish the top with whipped topping and add malted milk balls that have been crushed.

# Baked Apples With Raisins

Apple lovers who like baked goodies will certainly love this. This recipe serves 6.

Ingredients:

6 baking apples, cored

2 tablespoons butter

2 tablespoons brown sugar

1 tablespoon cinnamon

3 tablespoons rum

¼ cup honey

½ cup sultana raisins

½ cup water

1 tablespoon cornstarch

3 tablespoons cold water

Juice of 1 orange

Steps:
1. Preheat the oven to 350° Fahrenheit. Score the skin of the apples around the perimeter. Place the apples on a baking dish. Set these aside.
2. Cream the butter with the brown sugar in a bowl. Spoon this into the cavities of the apples using a small spoon. Stuff the cavities with cinnamon, rum, orange juice, raisins, and honey.
3. After stuffing the cavities, pour ½ cup water into the bottom of the baking dish.
4. Bake the apples for 40 minutes or until the apples become soft. The cooking time may actually depend on the type of apples you used. Check the apples from time to time to check if they are already cooked.
5. When cooked, remove the apples from the pan and set aside. Place the pan on the stove over medium heat. Cook the

liquid for 3 minutes. Dissolve the cornstarch in 3 tablespoons of cold water and stir into the cooling liquid. Cook this for 1 minute and serve with the apples.

6. You can serve the apples warm with ice cream if you like. You can also serve it with whipped topping, extra raisins, and other garnishes that you may like.

# Raw Vegan Snickers Bars

The Snickers bar is a common candy bar worldwide, but it also packs a lot of calories. Here's a healthier version of it. This can make 24 mini chocolates or 6 to 8 full-size chocolate bars.

Ingredients:

For the chocolate
- 1 cup virgin coconut oil
- ½ cup natural cocoa powder
- ¼ cup natural maple syrup

Caramel
- 1 cup dates, presoaked
- 3 tablespoons agave nectar
- 2 tablespoons almond butter
- ½ teaspoon sea salt
- 2 tablespoons coconut oil
- 1 ½ teaspoons vanilla extract

Extra ingredients
- 1 cup raw or dry roasted peanuts

Steps:

1. Put the 1 cup virgin coconut oil, half cup natural cocoa powder, and quarter of a cup natural maple syrup inside a food processor. Blend everything until the mixture becomes smooth. You may have to stop from time to time to scrape the sides down. Set this aside.

2. For the caramel, place the dates, agave nectar, almond butter, sea salt, coconut oil, and vanilla extract into the food processor and blend everything until the mixture becomes smooth. You may also have to stop from time to time to scrape down the sides of the processor.

3. Coat your muffin tin, mini muffin tin, or silicone molds with a thick layer of chocolate. This will help your chocolates to pop out quickly and easily.

4.  Layer in the caramel after the chocolate. You should then go in and top the caramel with peanuts. After that, you can add one final layer of the chocolate to coat and seal the top.
5.  Place this in the freezer to let everything set. This usually takes an hour.
6.  Remove the bars from the freezer and serve.

# White Chocolate-Ginger Milk Rice With Lime And Blueberries

Ingredients:

For the milk rice
- ☐ 100 grams short grain rice
- ☐ 400 ml milk
- ☐ 1 teaspoon vanilla paste, or
- ☐ 1 vanilla pod
- ☐ **1 lime**

White chocolate sauce
- ☐ 100 ml milk
- ☐ 100 ml cream
- ☐ 2 tablespoons of sugar
- ☐ **2 egg**
- ☐ 200 grams white chocolate
- ☐ ½ teaspoon of ground ginger
- ☐ **Blueberries**
- ☐ Coarsely chopped pistachio for garnish

Steps:
1. Bring the milk together with the vanilla paste to a boil in a saucepan. If using a vanilla pod, scrape the seeds from the pod first before mixing it with the milk.
2. Add in the rice and reduce the heat of the stove to love. Cook the rice with the lid on for about 30 to 35 minutes. Stir the rice once in a while to prevent it from sticking to the bottom.
3. When the rice is already cooked, remove it from the heat and add in the zest of a lime.
4. As for the sauce, warm the milk and the cream.
5. Whisk the egg yolks and sugar till the mixture becomes pale in color.
6. When the milk and cream mixture reaches 85°Celsius, place some of the mixture into the egg mixture while stirring constantly. This will temper the eggs and prevent them from getting cooked in lumps (like scrambled eggs).

7. Whisk in the egg mixture into the milk mixture and keep on stirring for about 2 minutes. Set this aside and add the ground ginger and chopped chocolate.
8. Let this stand for a minute or two, until the chocolate starts to melt. Stir everything until it becomes smooth.
9. Stir about half of the sauce into the milk rice. Warm the blueberries with lime juice and sugar, but do not cook them. Once the sugar is molten, remove it from the heat.
10. Serve the milk rice with the blueberries, topped with the remaining sauce and some coarsely chopped pistachio.

# Fruit Whole Wheat Crumble

You will need:

☐ 2 and a half cups of diced fresh fruits (whatever is in season), or canned fruit cocktail or a combination of other canned fruits of your choice.

☐ Two to three tablespoons of honey

☐ 2 tablespoons of raisins immersed in 2 tablespoons of fresh orange juice

For the crumble topping:

A couple of crushed granola bars

One 200g pack of whole wheat pancake mix

How to do it:

1. Mix fruits and honey in a bowl. Add the soaked raisins and toss well.
2. Distribute equal portions into ramekins or dessert dishes. Chill and set aside.
3. Prepare the crumble topping by starting with the pancake mix (cooked according to package instructions).
4. Use a few pancakes and crumble. Combine with crushed granola bars and toast slightly on a skillet.
5. Generously top the fruit mixture with the granola and pancake mixture. Drop a dollop of yogurt or whipped cream.

# Cherry Chocolate Baked Fauxlaska

**Ingredients:**

- ¾ cups cherry jam or preserves (homemade or your preferred brand)
- 4 large scoops chocolate ice cream (your preferred brand)
- 3 egg whites
- 6 tbsp caster sugar

**Directions:**

1. Set your broiler to heat. Between 4 custard cups or large ramekins, divide cherry preserves and top with a scoop of ice cream apiece. Set aside in freezer.
2. Beat egg whites in a stand mixer, with electric beater, or briskly by hand until soft and peaky; add caster sugar and continue beating until peaks become stiff and shiny.
3. Spoon dollops of egg whites on top ice cream, place under broiler for about 90 seconds, until golden brown. Serve immediately.

# Cocoa-Graham Snackwiches

**Ingredients:**

- 4 Graham cracker sheets
- 6 tbsp chocolate frosting or Nutella (homemade or your preferred brand)

**Directions:**

1. Halve each Graham cracker sheet along the crosswise sea. Spread one half of each cracker with 1½ tablespoon of frosting.
2. Top with other half.
3. Enjoy immediately or in a sack lunch.

# Chocolate-Banana Freeze

**Ingredients:**

- 2 bananas (fully yellow, but not overripe)
- ¾ cup dark or semisweet chocolate (chopped or chips)
- 2 tbsp canola or vegetable oil

**Directions**:

4. Line a flat baking dish with parchment or foil; set aside. Halve bananas and firmly insert a popsicle stick or the tines of a plastic fork into the cut end of each half. Arrange on baking sheet and place in freezer for 10-15 minutes.
5. Place chocolate bits in a microwave-safe dish, drizzle with oil, and microwave until smooth, stopping to to stir every 20 seconds.
6. Coat each banana half in melted chocolate and return to freezer until chocolate hardens and serve.

# Chocolate Crunchies

**Ingredients:**

- ⅔ cup chocolate chips or chunks
- 1 tbsp honey
- ¼ cup butter
- 1/3 cup cornflakes

**Directions:**

1. Arrange paper liners in the wells of a mini muffin tin. Place chocolate bits in a microwave-safe bowl with honey and butter. Microwave until smooth, stopping every 15-20 seconds to stir briskly.
2. Bit by bit, add cornflakes to melted chocolate mixture and stir to coat. Transfer into mini muffin tins, let cool in refrigerator for 10-15 minutes.

# Chocolate Dipped Potato Chips

**Ingredients:**

- 1 lb chocolate (chips or chopped to bits)
- 8 cups potatoes (ridged, thick-cut)

**Directions:**

1. Line baking sheets with waxed paper. Use a double boiler to melt ¾ of the chocolate, stirring regularly until just thoroughly melted, taking care not to scorch.
2. Remove melted chocolate from heat and whisk in remaining chocolate until melted.
3. Use tongs to dip potato chips one by one into melted chocolate; transfer in a single layer onto prepared baking sheets. Let set until chocolate hardens or place in fridge 5-10 minutes before enjoying.

# Chocolate Pudding Pie

**Ingredients:**

- 1 prepared chocolate Graham cracker crust
- 1 package instant chocolate pudding (your preferred brand and flavor)
- ¾ cup semi-sweet mini chocolate chips
- ¾ cup milk
- 2 cups prepared whipped cream

**Directions:**

1. Scatter chocolate chips evenly in the bottom of prepared crust. Whip pudding mix and milk until it begins to set, pour into crust and spread even.
2. Chill in refrigerator 15 minutes.
3. Top with whipped cream, slice, and serve.

# Chocolate Silk Whip

**Ingredients:**

- 1 cup semi-sweet chocolate chips
- ½ cup milk (whole)
- 3 egg whites
- 3 tbsp sugar

**Directions:**

1. Whisk together milk and sugar in a saucepan over medium setting until hot but not boiling. Place chocolate in a food processor or blender and pulse until chopped into finer bits.
2. Pour milk mixture over chocolate bits while running processor or blender and high speed.
3. Add egg whites while continuing to whip; continue whipping for 90 seconds.
4. Pour into 3-4 dessert dishes, cover, and place in refrigerator to chill.

# Chocolate Toffee Chunks

**Ingredients:**

- 4 cups semi-sweet chocolate chips
- 2 sticks butter (unsalted)
- 2 cups light brown sugar (packed)
- 1 cup walnuts (roughly chopped)

**Directions:**

1. Lightly grease a rimmed baking sheet and set aside. Melt together butter and brown sugar in a medium saucepan, whisking occasionally until boiling; lower heat and let simmer for 8-10 minutes, stirring vigilantly.
2. Remove saucepan from heat, stir in chopped walnuts, and immediately pour mixture onto prepared baking sheet; set aside.
3. Place chocolate in a microwave safe bowl; heat at half strength in 20 second intervals, stirring between each interval, until smooth and melted. Pour over toffee layer and smooth. Let set until hard, break into pieces, and enjoy.

# Chocolate Whipped Cream

**Ingredients:**

- ¼ cup cocoa (unsweetened)
- ½ cup powdered sugar
- 4½ cups heavy whipping cream (chilled)

**Directions:**

1. In a small bowl, sift together cocoa and sugar.
2. Chill a metal bowl and metal whisk in freezer. Pour cream into chilled bowl and whisk briskly until it begins to thicken. Add sifted cocoa and sugar mixture and continue whisking until completely set. Serve immediately.

# Chunky Chocolate Bark

**Ingredients:**

- 1 bag chocolate chips (milk, semi-sweet, dark, white – your preference)
- assorted toppings: chopped nuts, dried fruit, toasted seeds, cereal, candied ginger

**Directions:**

1. Chill a rimmed baking sheet in the freezer, lined with parchment.
2. Melt chocolate in a double boiler (or in a microwave, stopping every 20 seconds to stir until smooth). Remove baking sheet from freezer, pour on warm chocolate, spread evenly, sprinkle with chosen toppings, and return to freezer for 15-20 minutes.
3. Break set chocolate bar into large pieces and enjoy.

# Cinnamon-Spiced Hot Cocoa

**Ingredients:**

- 2½ cups milk
- 3 tbsp baking cocoa
- 4 tbsp sugar
- ½ tsp vanilla extract
- ¼ tsp cinnamon

**Directions:**

1. Whisk together cocoa, sugar, and cinnamon in a small saucepan.
2. Slowly stir milk into cocoa mixture over medium heat. Bring to temperature without boiling
3. Remove saucepan from heat, add vanilla, and whisk until frothy.
4. Pour into mugs and serve immediately.

# Cocoa- Amaretto Crepes

**Ingredients:**

- 1½ cups flour (all-purpose)
- ½ cup sugar
- ¼ cup baking cocoa
- 1½ cups milk (whole)
- 3 eggs
- 3 tbsp water
- 2 tsp vanilla extract
- pinch salt
- 1 cup cream cheese (room temperature)
- ½ cup sour cream
- ⅓ cup amaretto
- 1 cup whipped topping (room temperature)

**Directions:**

1. In a medium mixing bowl, whisk together flour, ¼ cup sugar, cocoa, milk, eggs, water, 1½ tsp vanilla, and salt. Set in refrigerator while you prepare filling.
2. In a separate medium bowl, beat together cream cheese and remaining sugar until fluffy Add sour cream and remaining vanilla, continuing to beat. Fold amaretto and whipped topping into mixture. Cover and place in refrigerator to chill for 30 minutes.
3. Lightly grease a medium, non-stick skillet and heat over medium. Pour 2-3 tablespoons of batter into center of skillet, immediately tilting and swirling the pan to spread batter in a thin pancake. When batter appears dry on top (about 45 seconds-1 minute), gently flip and cook an

additional 15-20 minutes. Transfer to a warm, covered plate. Repeat with remaining batter.
4. Run ¼ cup of filling down the middle of each crepe, roll, plate, and serve.

# Cocoa Rice Pudding

**Ingredients:**
- 1 cup instant rice
- 4 cups milk (whole)
- 1 package instant chocolate pudding
- ¼ tsp cinnamon
- 1 egg (beaten)

**Directions:**
1. Bring all ingredients to a boil in a medium saucepan. Remove from heat to cool 5-10 minutes, transfer to dessert bowls, and place in refrigerator to chill completely before serving.

# Cocoanut Candies

**Ingredients:**
- 2 lbs powdered sugar
- 2 sticks butter (room temperature)
- 1 cup coconut flakes
- 1 cup walnuts or pecans (chopped)
- 6 tbsp cream
- 2¼ cups chocolate chips
- 3 ounces paraffin cake

**Directions:**
1. Line a baking sheet with parchment. Use electric beaters or stand mixer to beat together powdered sugar, butter, coconut, chopped nuts, and cream. Form 2 tablespoon scoops of mixture into balls, place on prepared baking sheet, and chill.
2. While balls chill, melt together chocolate and paraffin in a medium saucepan, stirring frequently.
3. Dip prepared balls in chocolate and return to parchment; return dipped balls to refrigerator and let chill until set.

# Flourless Chocolate Torte

**Ingredients:**
- 2 cups baking chocolate (semi-sweet)
- 2 sticks butter (unsalted)
- 8 eggs
- $1/8$ tsp salt
- 1½ cups sugar

**Directions:**
1. Set your oven to heat to 350°F. Lightly grease a 10" Springform pan and set aside.
2. In a small saucepan, over low heat, melt together chocolate and butter. Remove from heat and blend in salt. Set aside to cool.
3. Separate eggs, placing whites in a large bowl and yolks in a separate medium mixing bowl.
4. Beat egg whites until stiff and peaky.
5. Add sugar to the egg yolk and beat thoroughly until mixture is thick, smooth, and pale yellow.
6. Fold ⅓ of the chocolate mixture into the sugar and yolk mixture. Transfer ⅓ of the beaten egg whites into the yolk and chocolate mixture and gently fold together.
7. Fold remaining chocolate mixture into batter then gently fold in remaining egg whites.
8. Pour batter into prepared pan and bake on middle rack for 30 minutes. Edges will be set, but the center will still be gelatinous when hot.
9. Cool to room temperature, then cover and refrigerate overnight, at least 8 hours.

# Fudgy Brownies

**Ingredients:**
- 1 cup flour (all-purpose)
- ½ cup baking chocolate
- 1½ sticks butter
- 2 cups sugar
- 3 eggs (beaten)
- 1½ tsp vanilla
- 1 cup chocolate chips

**Directions:**
1. Set your oven to heat to 350°F. Line a 9x13" baking dish with foil and set aside.
2. In a microwave-safe bowl, melt together baking chocolate and butter, stopping every 20 seconds to stir, until mixture is smooth. Add sugar to mixture and beat until thoroughly combined. Add eggs and combine in the same way. Stir in flour, vanilla, and chocolate chips.
3. Spread better in prepared baking dish, bake 30-35 minutes, let cook 20 minutes, slice, and serve.

# Grilled Chocowich

**Ingredients:**
- 8 slices whole wheat sandwich bread
- ¼ cup evaporated milk (nonfat)
- 3 ounces bittersweet chocolate (finely chopped)
- 1½ ounces semisweet chocolate chips
- 1½ tbsp butter (room temperature)

**Directions:**
1. In a small saucepan, heat evaporated milk just to boiling; remove from heat, add bittersweet chocolate, and whisk until melted and smooth.
2. While chocolate mixture cools slightly, butter one side of each bread slice. On un-buttered side of 4 slices, spread chocolate mixture evenly. Sprinkle with chocolate chips. Top with remaining bread slices, buttered side up.
3. Place a large, nonstick skillet over medium heat. Toast both sides of each sandwich until golden and chocolate chips are just melted. Serve immediately.

# Hot Fudge Sauce

**Ingredients:**
- 1¾ cup sugar
- 1 cup light brown sugar (packed)
- 1 cup cocoa powder (unsweetened)
- 4 tbsp flour
- ⅔ cup butter (unsalted, room temperature)
- 1½ cups water
- ½ tsp salt
- ½ tsp vanilla extract

**Directions:**
1. In a medium saucepan, whisk together sugar, brown sugar, cocoa, flour, and salt. Pour in water, add butter, and slowly bring to a boil. Boil mixture for 10 minutes, taking care to stir occasionally. Remove from stovetop, stir in vanilla, and serve over ice cream or as a dip for fruit or pretzels.

# Indoor S'mores

**Ingredients:**
- 4 Graham cracker squares
- 4 marshmallows
- 2 tbsp chocolate chips

**Directions:**
1. Placing an oven rack at the top, preheat your broiler. Arrange Graham crackers on a baking sheet, top each with 1 marshmallow, and broil 1-1½ minutes with the oven door ajar; watch marshmallows carefully and remove as soon as they turn golden brown.
2. In a small, microwave-safe bowl, microwave chocolate chips. Pause microwave every 7-10 seconds to stir until chips are melted smooth.
3. Drizzle melted chocolate over toasted marshmallow and serve.

# Miracle Mousse

**Ingredients:**
- ½ cup 70% dark chocolate solids (chopped)
- 1¼ cup heavy cream
- ¼ cup caster sugar
- 1 egg white

**Directions:**
1. Heat half of the cream just to boiling in a medium saucepan; turn off stovetop and whisk in chocolate pieces until completely melted and smooth.
2. Transfer mixture to a metal or glass bowl set in ice; add remaining cream and use electric beaters to beat mixture until soft peaks form. Remove bowl from ice and set aside.
3. In a separate bowl, beat egg white until stiff and peaky; slowly add sugar, beating until peaks are stiff and shiny.
4. Fold egg mixture gently into chocolate mixture, dollop into chilled dessert cups, and serve.

# Mud Pie

**Ingredients:**
- 1 prepared chocolate Graham cracker crust
- ½ cup cream cheese (room temperature)
- ½ cup sugar
- 1 tsp vanilla extract
- ⅓ cup cocoa powder (unsweetened)
- ⅓ cup milk (whole)
- 1 cup whipped topping (thawed)
- 1 cup whipping cream
- ¼ cup powdered sugar
- 2 tbsp chocolate shavings

**Directions:**
1. In a medium bowl, beat together cream cheese, sugar, vanilla, cocoa powder, and milk until smooth; fold whipped topping into mixture, spread evenly in prepared Graham crust, and place in freezer until firm.
2. Beat whipped cream and powdered sugar in a medium bowl until thick and fluffy. Spread over top of pie, sprinkle with chocolate shavings, slice, and serve.

# Mug O' Chocolate Cake

**Ingredients:**
- 4 tbsp flour (all-purpose)
- 4 tbsp sugar
- 2 tbsp cocoa (unsweetened)
- 1 egg
- 3 tbsp milk
- 3 tbsp canola or vegetable oil
- 2 drops vanilla extract
- 1 scoop ice cream

**Directions:**
1. In a standard-size coffee mug, stir together flour, sugar, and cocoa. Beat egg into flour mixture; add milk, oil, and vanilla and stir together thoroughly with a fork.
2. Place mug of batter in the microwave and cook on high for 3 minutes. Set aside to cool for 1-2 minutes, run a knife around the inside edge of the mug, upend over a bowl until cake slides out, top with ice cream, and enjoy.

# No-Bake Chocolate Wafer Cake

**Ingredients:**
- 2 cups heavy whipping cream
- 1 tsp vanilla extract
- 1½ cup chocolate wafer cookies (your preferred brand)
- 2 tbsp chocolate shavings

**Directions:**
1. Beat cream and vanilla together until thick, fluffy, and able to form stiff peaks.
2. Layer cookies and ½" cream until stacked 14" high; gentle lay on its side and coat with remaining whipped cream. Refrigerate.
3. Sprinkle with chocolate shavings, slice, and serve.

# Peanutty Chocolate Pizza

**Ingredients:**
- 2 cups prepared chocolate chip cookie dough (your preferred brand)
- ½ cup chocolate chips
- ½ cup chocolate peanut butter cup candies (roughly chopped)
- ½ peanut butter candies

**Directions:**
1. Set your oven to heat to 350°F. Press cookie dough evenly into a 9x13" baking dish and bake 15 minutes, until golden.
2. Remove from oven and immediately sprinkle with chocolate chips; let chips soften 1-2 minutes, then spread evenly over cookie "crust" before sprinkling with both candies. Slice and serve.

# Peppperminty Brownies

**Ingredients:**
- 1¼ cups flour (all-purpose)
- 1½ sticks butter (unsalted)
- ½ tsp salt
- ½ cup unsweetened chocolate (finely chopped)
- ½ cup semi-sweet chocolate (finely chopped)
- 2 cups sugar
- 1 tbsp vanilla extract
- 5 eggs (beaten)
- 20-14 peppermint patty candies

**Directions:**
1. Set your oven to heat to 350°F. Lightly grease a 9x13" baking dish and set aside.
2. Whisk together flour and salt in a medium bowl and set aside.
3. Melt butter and both chocolates together until smooth in a large saucepan, stirring often. Remove from stovetop, add sugar and vanilla, and whisk thoroughly. Beat eggs into chocolate mixture then stir in flour until just combined.
4. Pour half of chocolate batter into prepared dish, place peppermint patty candies in a even layer across the top, and spread with an even layer of the remaining batter.
5. Bake 30 minutes on middle rack; let cool 20 minutes before slicing and serving.

# Part 2

# 3d Chocolate Cheesecake

"This cheesecake deserves to earn a title of "3D". It's dark, deep, and decadent and always looks elegant because of the ganache coating. You'll love this version!"
Serving: 16 servings. | Prep: 30m | Ready in: 01h25m

Ingredients
- 1 cup chocolate graham cracker crumbs (about 5 whole crackers)
- 1 tbsp. sugar
- 1/4 cup butter, melted
- FILLING:
- 4 packages (8 oz. each) cream cheese, softened
- 1-1/3 cups sugar
- 1 package (10 oz.) 60% cacao bittersweet chocolate baking chips, melted and cooled
- 1/4 cup baking cocoa
- 4 large eggs, lightly beaten
- GANACHE:
- 2/3 cup (4 oz.) 60% cacao bittersweet chocolate baking chips
- 1/2 cup heavy whipping cream
- 1 tbsp. sugar

Direction
- Set the oven to 325°F for preheating. Grease a 9-inches springform pan and place it over a double thickness of heavy-duty foil, about 18-inches square, wrapping the foil tightly around the pan.

- Mix the sugar and cracker crumbs in a small bowl. Add in butter before pouring the mixture into the greased pan. Place the pan on a baking sheet and bake for 10 minutes. Transfer on a wire rack to cool.

- Whisk sugar and cream cheese in a big bowl until smooth. Mix in cooled chocolate and cocoa. Beat in eggs and whisk at low speed just until combined. Spread the mixture over the crust. Place the pan over a big baking pan with an inch of boiling water.

- Let it bake inside the oven for 55-60 minutes until the cake's top looks dull and its center is fixed. Remove the pan from the water bath and remove also its foil. Place the springform pan on a wire rack and allow it to cool for 10 minutes. Use a knife to loosen the edges of the cake. Cool for 60 more minutes. Store it inside the fridge overnight.

- Put the chocolate in a small bowl. For the ganache, boil cream and sugar in a small saucepan. Add the chocolate and mix until smooth. Let it cool, stirring for some time until the mixture reaches its spreading consistency.

- Remove the cheesecake from the pan. Drizzle ganache over the cheesecake to within 1-inch of edge. Store it inside the fridge for 1 hour until it's well-fixed.

Nutrition Information
- Calories: 480 calories
- Total Carbohydrate: 40 g
- Cholesterol: 133 mg
- Total Fat: 35 g
- Fiber: 2 g
- Protein: 8 g
- Sodium: 241 mg

# Apricot Cheesecake Tarts

""Made special for a springtime buffet with apricots and dark chocolate.""
Serving: 15 tartlets. | Prep: 30m | Ready in: 30m

Ingredients
- 3 oz. bittersweet chocolate, chopped
- 1/2 tsp. shortening
- 1 package (1.9 oz.) frozen miniature phyllo tart shells
- 3 oz. cream cheese, softened
- 2 tbsps. confectioners' sugar
- 2 tbsps. sour cream
- 2 tsps. apricot nectar
- 3 dried apricots, cut into thin strips
- 1 to 1-1/2 tsps. grated chocolate

Direction
- Place shortening and bittersweet chocolate in a microwave to melt; mix until it turns smooth. Sweep over the bottom and up sides of tart shells. Place inside the refrigerator for 15 minutes or until chocolate is set. In the meantime, beat confectioners' sugar and cream cheese in a small bowl until it turns smooth. Add in apricot nectar and sour cream. Scoop into shells. Let it chill for at least 20 minutes, covered. Place grated chocolate and apricot strips on top just before serving.

Nutrition Information
- Calories: 83 calories
- Total Carbohydrate: 7 g
- Cholesterol: 8 mg
- Total Fat: 6 g
- Fiber: 1 g
- Protein: 1 g
- Sodium: 28 mg

# Bittersweet Chocolate Cheesecake

""My whole family loves this dessert, and I am a great-grandmother. Got this recipe from my niece. Super chocolaty.""
Serving: 16 servings. | Prep: 20m | Ready in: 01h20m

Ingredients
- 1 cup chocolate wafer crumbs
- 1/2 cup finely chopped hazelnuts, toasted
- 1/3 cup butter, melted
- 3 packages (8 oz. each) cream cheese, softened
- 1 cup sugar
- 12 oz. bittersweet chocolate, melted and cooled
- 1 cup sour cream
- 1-1/2 tsps. vanilla extract
- 1/2 tsp. almond extract
- Dash salt
- 3 large eggs, lightly beaten
- GLAZE:
- 4 oz. bittersweet chocolate, chopped
- 1/4 cup heavy whipping cream
- 1 tsp. vanilla extract
- Whipped cream and additional toasted hazelnuts, optional

Direction
- Prepare the oven by preheating to 350°F. Combine melted butter, hazelnuts and wafer crumbs; then press onto bottom of a 9-inch springform pan that is not greased.

- Whip sugar and cream cheese until smooth. Mix in cooled chocolate, then salt, extracts and sour cream. Put in eggs; whisk on low speed just until just combined. Put over crust. Put the pan on a baking sheet.
- Bake for 60-65 minutes until middle is just set. Place on a wire rack to cool for 10 minutes. Use a knife to loosen sides from pan; cool for 1 more hour. Keep in the refrigerator for 3 hours.
- To make glaze, melt chocolate with cream in a microwave; whisk until smooth. Mix in vanilla. Put over chilled cheesecake and spread. Put in the refrigerator, covered, for overnight. Take off rim from pan. Served with additional hazelnuts and whipped cream if wished.

Nutrition Information
- Calories: 484 calories
- Total Carbohydrate: 34 g
- Cholesterol: 112 mg
- Total Fat: 39 g
- Fiber: 3 g
- Protein: 8 g
- Sodium: 235 mg

# Black Forest Cheesecake

"This delicious cake has won a baking contest. Definitely worth the time to prepare it."

Serving: 10 | Prep: 1h | Ready in: 9h

Ingredients
- 1/2 cup semi-sweet chocolate chips
- 1/2 cup butter
- 1 cup graham cracker crumbs
- 1/3 cup brown sugar
- 1 tbsp. water
- 1 tsp. ground cinnamon
- 5 (8 oz.) packages cream cheese, softened
- 1 1/4 cups white sugar
- 5 eggs
- 1 tsp. vanilla extract
- 1/2 cup semi-sweet chocolate chips
- 1/2 (16 oz.) jar maraschino cherries - drained, chopped, and juices reserved
- 2 tsps. cornstarch
- 1/2 (16 oz.) jar maraschino cherries, halved
- 3 tbsps. semisweet chocolate chips

Direction
- Set oven to 500 degrees F or 260 degrees C and preheat. Fill a roasting pan halfway with water and place it at the bottom rack of the oven. Grease a 10-inch pie pan.

- In a microwave, heat half a cup butter and half a cup chocolate chips in a microwave-safe bowl for about 1 minute until melted. Stir to combine then add graham cracker crumbs, brown sugar, cinnamon and water; stir. Press the cracker mix into the bottom of a greased 10-inch pie pan and about 1 inch up the sides. Put pan aside.
- In a large bowl, beat with an electric mixer the white sugar and cream cheese until light and fluffy. Drop in eggs one at a time. Before adding the next egg, make sure that the previous one has been thoroughly blended into the cream cheese mixture. Beat in the vanilla with the last egg. Set aside a third of the cream cheese mixture in a bowl. Pour the remaining two-thirds of batter into the prepared crust.
- Using a ceramic bowl or microwave-safe glass container, melt 1/2 cup chocolate chips using the microwave in 15-second intervals, stirring the chocolate after each melting, for 1-3 minutes, depending on your microwave. Observe carefully to avoid overheating and scorching the chocolate. Add the reserved cream cheese batter and mix well. Take the pan and pour the chocolate mixture on top of the white filling. To create a marbled look, run a knife decoratively through the filling. Sprinkle the top with chopped maraschino cherries. Put the pie pan on a baking sheet.
- Put on the top rack of the preheated oven. Bake for 10 minutes, then reduce heat to 200 degrees F or 95 degrees C. Continue baking for about 1 hour until you have a nicely puffed edges and the surface of the cheesecake is firm except for a small spot in the middle that will jiggle when the pan is shaken gently. Turn off the oven and leave the cheesecake to rest in the oven for 1 1/2 hours and keep the oven door closed. Using the tip of a paring knife, run around the edges of the pan. Transfer the pan on a wire rack and let the cheesecake cool at room temperature for 30 minutes. Refrigerate and cool for another 3 hours.

- Heat the reserved maraschino cherry juice and cornstarch in a saucepan, setting it on medium heat. Stir for 5 to 7 minutes until the sauce has thickened. Set it aside to cool completely then pour the cooked sauce over the cheesecake. Garnish top with halved cherries. Take the remaining 3 tbsps. chocolate chip and melt it in a microwave-safe bowl in 15 second intervals, stirring after each melting. Drizzle the chocolate syrup on top of the cheesecake. Refrigerate for at least 2 hours more before serving.

Nutrition Information
- Calories: 815 calories;
- Total Carbohydrate: 68.3 g
- Cholesterol: 229 mg
- Total Fat: 57.4 g
- Protein: 12.8 g
- Sodium: 483 mg

# Black Forest Cheesecakes

""These simple mini-cheesecakes combine the perfect match of cherries and chocolate for a Yuletide treat.""
Serving: 12 | Prep: 20m | Ready in: 2h40m

Ingredients
- 12 chocolate sandwich cookies with creme filling
- 2 (8 oz.) packages cream cheese, softened
- 3/4 cup white sugar
- 1/3 cup baking cocoa
- 1 tsp. vanilla extract
- 2 eggs
- 1 (21 oz.) can cherry pie filling
- 1/2 cup whipped topping

Direction
- Prepare the oven by preheating to 325°F (160°C). Use paper or foil muffin liners to line muffin cups.
- Take off the cookie top from each sandwich cookie; crush and reserve. Put cream-topped cookies in lined muffin cups, cream side up.
- Use an electric mixer to beat vanilla extract, baking cocoa, sugar and cream cheese in a large bowl until fluffy. Stir in eggs until combined. Then fill prepared muffin cups 3/4 full; sprinkle 1/4 cup reserved cookie crumbs over the top. Get rid of remaining crumbs or keep for another use.

- Place in the preheated oven and bake for 20-25 minutes until set. Fully cool; keep in the refrigerator, covered for at least 2 hours.
- Place 2 tbsps. pie filling on top of each cheesecake and a dollop of whipped topping just before serving.

Nutrition Information
- Calories: 307 calories;
- Total Carbohydrate: 36.3 g
- Cholesterol: 74 mg
- Total Fat: 16.7 g
- Protein: 5.1 g
- Sodium: 183 mg

# Blissful Peanut Butter-Chocolate Cheesecake

"The three words that best describe this cheesecake are fun, delicious, and decadent. Just try one bite and you'll agree to this description."

Serving: 12 servings. | Prep: 60m | Ready in: 02h00m

Ingredients
- 32 Nutter Butter cookies
- 1/3 cup butter, melted
- 4 packages (8 oz. each) cream cheese, softened
- 1 cup sugar
- 3 oz. semisweet chocolate, melted
- 3 oz. bittersweet chocolate, melted
- 1 tsp. vanilla extract
- 4 eggs, lightly beaten
- PEANUT BUTTER MOUSSE:
- 1-1/2 tsps. unflavored gelatin
- 2 tbsps. cold water
- 1 cup heavy whipping cream
- 3 tbsps. creamy peanut butter
- 2 tbsps. sugar
- 2 egg yolks
- GARNISH:
- 3 oz. semisweet chocolate, chopped
- Chocolate curls and sweetened whipped cream, optional

Direction

- Place a greased 9-inches springform pan over an 18-inch double thick and heavy-duty square shaped foil. Wrap the foil tightly around the pan.
- Grind the cookies in a food processor until it appears fine crumbs. Mix in butter. Pour the mixture into the bottom and 2-inches up the sides of the greased pan. Set aside the pan.
- Whisk sugar and cream cheese in a big bowl until smooth. Stir in vanilla and melted chocolates. Whisk in eggs and beat at low speed until the egg incorporates. Spread the mixture over the crust. Place the pan in a big baking pan with an inch of hot water.
- Set the oven to 325°F and bake for 60-65 minutes until the top appears dull and the center is fixed. Remove the pan from the water bath and transfer it into a wire rack. Cool for 10 minutes. Loosen the sides of the cheesecake using a knife. Cool for 60 more minutes.
- To make a peanut butter moose, add gelatin on cold water. Set aside for 60 seconds. Place it inside the microwave and heat on the high setting for 20 to 30 seconds. Whisk and set aside for 60 seconds until the gelatin dissolves completely.
- Heat peanut butter, sugar, and cream in a small and heavy saucepan until bubbles appear on the sides of the pan. Add a bit of the hot mixture in egg yolks. Bring the mixture back into the pan and constantly stir.
- Cook the mixture on low heat, stirring constantly until it has a thick consistency and when it coats the back of the spoon. Add the gelatin mixture. Transfer the heated mixture immediately in a bowl. Place it in ice water and whisk for 15 minutes until the mixture is thick and cold. Spread the mixture over the cheesecake. Store it inside the fridge overnight. Remove the rim from the pan.
- Melt chocolate in a microwave. Spread the melted chocolate over the cheesecake. Style the cake with whipped cream and chocolate curls.

Nutrition Information
- Calories: 792 calories
- Total Carbohydrate: 58 g
- Cholesterol: 228 mg
- Total Fat: 59 g
- Fiber: 2 g
- Protein: 15 g
- Sodium: 448 mg

# Blossom Cheesecake

""This bright bloom is sure to turn to everyone's favorite with awesome taste and delectable decorations! Plus, it's simpler make to than you might know. After baking a creamy white chocolate cheesecake, our crafty staff combined white and pink candy coating. And they brushed onto edible leaves and allow to firm, making petal shapes. To complete, our cooks colored additional candy-coating yellow for the flower's center and pile the pieces on top of the dessert. You could simply do the same, just follow the instructions here!""
Serving: 12-14 servings. | Prep: 60m | Ready in: 01h55m

Ingredients
- CRUST:
- 1-1/2 cups graham cracker crumbs (about 24 squares)
- 1 cup quick-cooking oats
- 1/4 cup sugar
- 1/2 cup butter, melted
- FILLING:
- 3 packages (8 oz. each) cream cheese, softened
- 1 cup sugar
- 3 tsps. vanilla extract
- 16 oz. white baking chocolate, melted and cooled
- 4 egg whites
- 1/8 tsp. cream of tartar
- 1/8 tsp. salt
- 1 tbsp. confectioners' sugar
- TOPPING:
- 2 cups (16 oz.) sour cream

- 2 tbsps. sugar
- 3 tsps. vanilla extract
- DECORATIONS:
- 9 oz. white candy coating, divided
- 8 oz. pink candy coating disks
- Yellow gel food coloring
- Lemon or rose leaves that have not been treated with chemicals
- Small pastry brush or new paint brush

Direction
- Mix in a food processor the sugar, oats and cracker crumbs. Then cover and blend until it forms fine crumbs. Put the butter and blend well. Then press onto the bottom and 1-1/2 inch up the sides of a greased 10-inch springform pan. Put on a baking sheet. Bake in the oven for 8-10 minutes at 350°F or until golden brown in color. Put on a wire rack and cool.
- Beat vanilla, sugar and cream cheese in a large bowl until fluffy and light. Mix in the melted white chocolate just until combined.
- Whisk the salt, cream of tartar and egg whites in a separate bowl on medium speed until it forms soft peaks. Put in the confectioner's sugar, whisking on high until it forms stiff peaks. Add into chocolate mixture and fold. Put into crust. Move pan to a baking sheet. Bake in the oven for 45-55 minutes at 350°F or until middle is nearly set.
- Mix in a bowl the vanilla, sugar and sour cream. Then spread over the top of cheesecake. Bake for 10 more minutes. Place on a wire rack to cool for 10 minutes. Gently run a knife around the edge of the pan to loosen. Cool for 1 more hour. Keep in the refrigerator for overnight. Take off sides of the pan.
- BLOSSOM: Rinse rose leaves or lemon and reserve to dry.

- Reserve 1 oz. of white candy coating for flower center. Melt remaining white candy coating and the pink disks in a microwave. Mix until combined. Brush a thin even coat of the pink mixture onto the bottom side of each leaf using a pastry brush or new paint brush. Put leaves with coated side up on a waxed paper. Keep in the refrigerator for 10 minutes or until set.

- Then coat leaves with a second pink layer the same as before. Let it chill until set. Cautiously peel leaves away from pink petals. Keep in the refrigerator until ready to assemble.

- Melt reserved white candy coating. Mix in yellow food coloring until combined. Place into a 3-1/2-inch circle on waxed paper and spread. Keep in the refrigerator until set.

- ASSEMBLY: For flower center, take out yellow circle from waxed paper and put in the middle of the cheesecake.

- Based on the photo at left for position, lay out petals around the flower center, overlapping petals slightly and positioning larger ones at the outside.

- Put the cheesecake on a cake plate.

# Brownie Cheesecake

"Mixing crumbled brownies into the batter before baking adds luscious experience on the silky and rich chocolate cheesecake."
Serving: 10-12 servings. | Prep: 20m | Ready in: 01h10m

Ingredients
- 1-1/2 cups crushed vanilla wafers (about 45 wafers)
- 6 tbsps. confectioners' sugar
- 6 tbsps. baking cocoa
- 6 tbsps. butter, melted
- FILLING:
- 3 packages (8 oz. each) cream cheese, softened
- 1/4 cup butter, melted
- 1/2 cup baking cocoa
- 4 eggs, lightly beaten
- 1 can (14 oz.) sweetened condensed milk
- 3 tsps. vanilla extract
- 1-1/2 cups crumbled brownies
- Whipped topping and pecan halves, optional

Direction
- Mix cocoa, confectioners' sugar, and wafer crumbs in a small bowl. Mix in butter. Put the mixture in a 9-inch greased springform pan and compress onto the bottom of the pan; reserve.
- Combine butter and cream cheese in a large bowl until the consistency is smooth. Mix in cocoa. While beating on low, add the eggs until just mixed. Slowly mix vanilla and milk in until just

mixed. Stir in brownies by folding. Scoop the filling on top of crust. Put the springform pan on a baking sheet.

• Place inside the oven and bake at 350°F until the middle part has almost set, about 50-55 minutes. Transfer to a wire rack and let cool for 10 minutes. Loosen from the pan by cautiously running a knife around its sides. Let the cheesecake cool for 1 hour more. Leave overnight inside the refrigerator.

• Decorate cheesecake with pecans and whipping cream if you want. Store leftovers in refrigerator.

# Brownie Swirl Cheesecake

"The secret of this elegant looking cheesecake is from this packaged brownie mix. The recipe is just so simple, and you can even add some chocolate swirls on top."
Serving: 8-10 servings. | Prep: 10m | Ready in: 60m

Ingredients
- 1 package (8 oz.) brownie mix
- 2 packages (8 oz. each) cream cheese, softened
- 1/2 cup sugar
- 1 tsp. vanilla extract
- 2 large eggs
- 1 cup milk chocolate chips, melted
- Whipped cream and miniature chocolate kisses, optional

Direction
- Follow the package's instruction to prepare the brownie mix for fudge brownies that are chewy. Place it into a 9-inch springform pan that is greased. Let it bake at 350°F 15 minutes (if tested they should not be done). Let them cool on a wire rack for about 10 minutes.

- In the meantime, mix sugar, cream cheese and vanilla in a bowl. One by one, add eggs and beat after every addition.

- Spread on the brownie crust and top it with melted chocolate. Using a knife, swirl in chocolate by cutting through the batter.

- Let it bake at 350°F until the middle is nearly set, 35 to 40 minutes. Loosen cake from pan by running a knife around its edges. Let it cool completely before removing the pan's sides. Place it in the refrigerator for 3 or more hours. You can add some style by putting chocolate kisses and whipped cream on top.

Nutrition Information
- Calories: 314 calories
- Total Carbohydrate: 38 g
- Cholesterol: 72 mg
- Total Fat: 17 g
- Fiber: 1 g
- Protein: 5 g
- Sodium: 182 mg

# Butterfinger Cheesecake

""I love cheesecake! I knew this recipe was for me when I found it featuring Butterfinger candy bars. Every one asked me to share this one so they could make it to excite a family back home. They couldn't believe something so delicate-looking was so simple to make.""

Serving: 12 servings. | Prep: 45m | Ready in: 01h45m

Ingredients
- 2 cups chocolate wafer crumbs (about 35 wafers)
- 1/3 cup butter, melted
- 4 packages (8 oz. each) cream cheese, softened
- 1 cup sugar
- 3 tbsps. heavy whipping cream
- 1-1/2 tsps. vanilla extract
- 5 large eggs, lightly beaten
- 3 Butterfinger candy bars (2.1 oz. each), frozen and chopped
- TOPPING:
- 1 Butterfinger candy bar (2.1 oz.), frozen and chopped
- 2 tbsps. butterscotch ice cream topping

Direction
- In a small bowl, mix the butter and wafer crumbs. Then press on the bottom and 1-1/2 in. on the sides of 9-inch springform pan that is greased; Let it rest. Put aside and then serve.
- Whisk sugar and cream cheese in a big bowl until smooth. Mix in vanilla and cream. Put in eggs; whisk on low speed until mixed. Add in chopped candy bars then fold. Place in crust. Transfer the pan to a baking sheet.

- Bake in the oven for 60 to 70 minutes at 325°F or until the middle is set. Place on wire rack to cool for 10 minutes.
- Cautiously run a knife around the edges of pan to loosen; cool for 1 more hour. Keep in the refrigerator overnight.
- Dust chopped candy bar on cheesecake; then pour butterscotch topping. Store leftovers in the refrigerator.

Nutrition Information
- Calories: 667 calories
- Total Carbohydrate: 62 g
- Cholesterol: 172 mg
- Total Fat: 44 g
- Fiber: 1 g
- Protein: 11 g
- Sodium: 509 mg

# Candy Bar Cheesecake

"Create exquisite cheesecake easily. One would think that it has been bought from a store."
Serving: 12-14 servings. | Prep: 25m | Ready in: 01h40m

Ingredients
- 1-3/4 cups crushed chocolate wafers (about 28 wafers)
- 1/4 cup sugar
- 1/3 cup butter, melted
- FILLING:
- 3 packages (8 oz. each) cream cheese, softened
- 1 can (14 oz.) sweetened condensed milk
- 1 cup chocolate syrup
- 2 tsps. vanilla extract
- 3 eggs, lightly beaten
- 6 Snickers candy bars (2.07 oz. each), coarsely chopped, divided
- Additional chocolate syrup

Direction
- Mix sugar and wafer crumbs in a small bowl. Mix butter in. In a greased 9-inch springform pan, pour mixture and compress onto the pan's base and 1-1/2 inches up each side of pan. Use heavy-duty foil (about 18-inch square) at double thickness to place the pan on. Wrap the foil around the pan firmly. On a baking sheet place the pan. Put inside the oven and bake for 12 minutes at 325°F. Move to a wire rack for cooling.

- Whip vanilla, chocolate syrup, milk and cream cheese in a large bowl until the texture is smooth. Put in egg; whip continuously until just mixed and add 2-1/2 cups of chopped candy bars. Place in crust. In a large pan with an inch of hot water, place the springform.

- Put inside the oven and bake for 75-80 minutes at 325°F or until the middle has just set and top appears dry. Take springform from the water bath. Transfer to a wire rack and let it cool for 10 minutes. Loosen the cake by running a knife cautiously around the pan's edges; let it cool for another 1 hour. Put inside refrigerator for a night.

- Add left chopped candy bars; add more chocolate syrup by drizzling.

Nutrition Information
- Calories: 347 calories
- Total Carbohydrate: 44 g
- Cholesterol: 85 mg
- Total Fat: 16 g
- Fiber: 1 g
- Protein: 6 g
- Sodium: 233 mg

# Candy Cane Cheesecake

""You can alter what you top this jolly cheesecake with: crushed candy canes are a must, but you can use whipped cream on top prior sprinkling with candy canes or pour with some dissolved chocolate chips. Do add your reviews as you find ways to improve this one!""

Serving: 12 | Prep: 30m | Ready in: 1day2h40m

Ingredients
- 1 cup chocolate cookie crumbs
- 3 tbsps. white sugar
- 1/4 cup butter, melted
- 4 (8 oz.) packages cream cheese, softened
- 2 tbsps. all-purpose flour
- 1/4 tsp. salt
- 1 3/4 cups white sugar
- 1/2 cup sour cream
- 2 1/2 tsps. vanilla extract, divided
- 3 eggs
- 1/2 tsp. peppermint extract
- 2 dashes red food coloring
- 1/2 cup crushed peppermint candies

Direction
- Prepare the oven by preheating to 400°F (200°C). Prepare a 9-inch springform pan that is lightly greased.
- In a bowl, mix 3 tbsps. of sugar and cookie crumbs. Then drizzle melted butter in the mixture while whisking until equally moistened. And press the mixture at the bottom of the pan.

- Place in the preheated oven and bake for 10 minutes until set; reserve to cool. Lower the oven's temperature to 300°F (150°C).

- In a big bowl, mix salt, flour and cream cheese. Use an electric hand mixer and beat on low speed until fluffy and smooth. Put in 1 1/2 tsp. vanilla, sour cream and 1 3/4 cup sugar and whisk until combined. Mix in eggs, one at a time, pausing and scraping down sides of the bowl between every egg.

- Split the mixture equally in two separate bowls. In a bowl, mix in 1 tsp. vanilla. Add the red food coloring mix and peppermint extract in the other bowl and blend until you achieve a reddish-pink color. Put more coloring as necessary. Switch layers of 1 cup each of the white and pink on the cooled crust until all filling is used.

- Put in the preheated oven and bake for 60 to70 minutes until filling is set. The middle will shake slightly once the pan is shaken and the edges will be puffed slightly.

- Dust the crushed candies equally over cheesecake and cautiously press on the top. Let it cool on a rack at room temperature. Then cover loosely and keep in the refrigerator overnight prior serving.

Nutrition Information
- Calories: 545 calories;
- Total Carbohydrate: 52.4 g
- Cholesterol: 143 mg
- Total Fat: 34.5 g
- Protein: 8.3 g
- Sodium: 378 mg

# Cannoli Cheesecake

""The airy ricotta filling with flecks of candied orange peel and chocolate chips sprinkled throughout makes for a perfect marriage of American and Italian.""
Serving: Makes 8 to 12 servings | Prep: 20m

Ingredients
- 4 (4 3/4-by 2 1/2-inch) graham crackers, crumbled
- 1/3 cup slivered almonds
- 3 tbsps. granulated sugar
- 1/2 stick unsalted butter, melted
- 1 3/4 cups (15 oz.) whole-milk ricotta
- 1/4 cup granulated sugar
- 1 tbsp. grated orange zest
- 1 large egg, separated
- 1/3 cup candied orange peel, chopped
- 1/3 cup semisweet chocolate chips, chopped
- 4 large egg whites
- 2 tsp. confectioners sugar
- Equipment: a 9-inch springform pan

Direction
- Preparation
- For Crust: Prepare the oven by preheating to 350°F with rack in center. Reverse bottom of springform pan and lock on the side.
- In a food processor, blend sugar, almonds, and graham cracker until ground, then place in a bowl. Mix in butter until blended.
- Then press crumb mixture equally on the bottom of a 1/2 inch up side of the pan. Put in the preheated oven and bake for 8

minutes. Let cool at room temperature for 15 minutes (still in pan). Keep oven on.

• For cheesecake: In a big bowl, mix the egg yolk, zest, granulated sugar, and ricotta until blended, then mix in chocolate chip and candied orange peel.

• Whisk all 5 egg whites and a pinch of salt in a separate bowl using an electric mixer until soft peaks form. Add into ricotta mixture and fold carefully but thoroughly.

• Transfer filling into crust and bake for 55 minutes to 1 hour until top is golden and puffed.

• Let cool in pan for 15 minutes. Use a knife to run around edges of pan to make the cake loose, then take off side of the pan. Let cool at room temperature for 1 hour. Sprinkle with confectioners' sugar.

• Chef's Note: You can chill cheesecake for 1 day, covered.

Nutrition Information
• Calories: 241

• Total Carbohydrate: 20 g

• Cholesterol: 52 mg

• Total Fat: 15 g

• Fiber: 1 g

• Protein: 8 g

• Sodium: 92 mg

• Saturated Fat: 8 g

# Cappuccino Cheesecake Pie

"This pie is delightful because of its attractive chocolate decorations and mocha filling, perfect for Valentine's Day and any occasion."

Serving: 8 servings. | Prep: 20m | Ready in: 60m

Ingredients
- 2 packages (8 oz. each) cream cheese, softened
- 1/2 cup sugar
- 1 envelope mocha cappuccino mix (1/4 cup)
- 2 eggs, lightly beaten
- 1/4 cup milk
- 1 extra-servings-size graham cracker crust (9 oz.)
- GARNISH:
- 1/4 cup semisweet chocolate chips
- 1/2 tsp. shortening

Direction
- Whip cappuccino mix, sugar, and cream cheese in a large bowl. Put in the milk and eggs; continue whipping until mixed well. Put in the crust.

- Place inside a 325°F oven and bake until the middle part is nearly set, about 40-45 minutes. Transfer to a wire rack to cool down for 1 hour. Put inside the refrigerator for 3 hours or for a night.

- Dissolve shortening and chocolate chips in a microwave; mix until the consistency is smooth. On a sheet of waxed paper, pour the melted chocolate mixture and evenly distribute into a 4-inch square. Place chocolate in room temperature, and let it set for 1 hour.

• Cut out eight chocolate hearts using a cookie cutter that is heart-shaped. Sprinkle with a heart each cooking. Keep remaining cookies in refrigerator.

# Caramel Chocolate Cheesecake Bites

""The wheat germ creates getting these yummy bites a snap to get out of the pan. They're delightful and a favorite all the time.""

Serving: 3 dozen. | Prep: 15m | Ready in: 30m

Ingredients
- 3/4 cup toasted wheat germ
- 2 packages (8 oz. each) reduced-fat cream cheese
- 3/4 cup sugar
- 1/3 cup baking cocoa
- 4 egg whites
- 1 tsp. vanilla extract
- 36 pecan halves
- 3 tbsps. fat-free caramel ice cream topping

Direction
- Use cooking spray to grease 36 miniature muffin cups; coat each using wheat germ well. Put aside.
- Beat sugar and cream cheese in a big bowl until it turns smooth. Put in cocoa; blend well. Mix in vanilla and eggs until blended. Place 4 tsps. into every muffin cup.
- Put in the oven and bake for 13 to16 minutes at 350°F or until set. Let cool in pans for 10 minutes before transferring to wire racks. Let cool for 30 minutes and put in the refrigerator. (Cheesecake might sink in the middle while cooling). To serve, put a pecan half on each top. Put caramel topping in a microwave for 10 seconds on high or until soft. Put 1/4 tsp. on each.

Nutrition Information
- Calories: 147 calories
- Total Carbohydrate: 15 g
- Cholesterol: 12 mg
- Total Fat: 8 g
- Fiber: 1 g
- Protein: 5 g
- Sodium: 136 mg

# Caramel Fudge Cheesecake

"This recipe will satisfy both the chocolate lovers and cheesecake lovers in the family. The combination of chocolaty cheesecake, crunchy pecans, fudgy crust and gooey layer of caramel makes this dessert very hard to resist."
Serving: 12 servings. | Prep: 30m | Ready in: 01h05m

Ingredients
- 1 package fudge brownie mix (8-inch square pan size)
- 1 package (14 oz.) caramels
- 1/4 cup evaporated milk
- 1-1/4 cups coarsely chopped pecans
- 2 packages (8 oz. each) cream cheese, softened
- 1/2 cup sugar
- 2 large eggs, lightly beaten
- 2 oz. unsweetened chocolate, melted and cooled

Direction
- Prepare the brownie batter according to package directions. Spread evenly into a greased 9-in. springform pan. Place the pan on a baking sheet then bake for 20 minutes at 350 degrees. Remove from oven and transfer to a wire rack to cool for 10 minutes. Keep the oven on.
- In a microwave-safe bowl, melt the caramels with milk. Pour melted caramel over the brownie crust and sprinkle with pecans
- In a large bowl, bring together sugar and cream cheese and beat until it's light and fluffy. Add eggs and continue beating on low speed just to combine the mixture. Add in melted chocolate and stir. Pour the mixture over pecans then return the pan into the baking sheet.

- Bake for 35 to 40 minutes or until the center is nearly set. Take the pan out of the oven and move onto a wire rack, cool for 10 minutes. Loosen the edge of the pan by running a knife around the edge and cool for another 1 hour. Refrigerate cheesecake overnight. Remove sides of the pan before serving.

Nutrition Information
- Calories: 635 calories
- Total Carbohydrate: 69 g
- Cholesterol: 90 mg
- Total Fat: 38 g
- Fiber: 3 g
- Protein: 10 g
- Sodium: 369 mg

# Caramel Stripe Cheesecake

""I enjoy baking cheesecakes, and this recipe is one of the best I've tried.""

Serving: 14 servings. | Prep: 35m | Ready in: 01h15m

Ingredients
- CRUST:
- 2 cups crushed vanilla wafers (about 60 wafers)
- 1/3 cup butter, melted
- FILLING:
- 3 packages (8 oz. each) cream cheese, softened
- 1 cup sugar
- 2 tbsps. all-purpose flour
- 2 tbsps. heavy whipping cream
- 1 tsp. vanilla extract
- 3 eggs, lightly beaten
- CARAMEL TOPPING:
- 12 caramels
- 2 tbsps. heavy whipping cream
- CHOCOLATE TOPPING:
- 1/2 cup semisweet chocolate chips
- 2 tsps. butter
- 4 tsps. heavy whipping cream
- Whipped cream and coarsely chopped pecans, optional

Direction
- Mix in a small bowl the butter and wafer crumbs. Then push down onto the bottom and 1-1/2-inch up the sides of an

ungreased 9-inch springform pan. Put on a baking sheet. Bake in the oven for 10 minutes at 400°F. Put the pan on a wire rack to cool. Lower heat to 350°F.

- Beat sugar and cream cheese in a large bowl until becomes smooth. Mix in the vanilla, cream and flour. Put in eggs; whisk on low speed just until mixed. Place into crust.

- Place in the oven and bake for 40-45 minutes or until middle is just set. Place on a wire rack to cool for 10 minutes. Cautiously run a knife around edge of pan to loosen; let cool for 1 more hour. Then chill while making the toppings.

- Melt caramels with cream over medium heat in a small saucepan, whisking constantly. Dissolve butter with cream and chocolate chips in a separate sauce over low heat, whisking until turns smooth. Then drizzle caramel and chocolate toppings over cheesecake. Keep for overnight in the refrigerator.

- Take off the sides of pan just before serving. Decorate with whipped cream and pecans if wished.

Nutrition Information
- Calories: 442 calories
- Total Carbohydrate: 40 g
- Cholesterol: 122 mg
- Total Fat: 30 g
- Fiber: 1 g
- Protein: 6 g
- Sodium: 283 mg

# Chilled Raspberry Cheesecake

"Save your romantic dinner with this delightful cheesecake."
Serving: 4 servings. | Prep: 20m | Ready in: 30m

Ingredients
- 3/4 cup crushed vanilla wafers (about 25 wafers)
- 3 tbsps. confectioners' sugar
- 3 tbsps. baking cocoa
- 3 tbsps. butter, melted
- 1 cup fresh or frozen raspberries, thawed
- 1-1/2 tsps. unflavored gelatin
- 1/2 cup cold water
- 1 package (8 oz.) cream cheese, softened
- 1/4 cup sugar
- 1/2 tsp. vanilla extract

Direction
- Mix wafer crumbs, cocoa, and confectioner's sugar in a bowl; add butter. Coat a 6-in. springform pan with cooking spray and press the mixture on bottom and 1-in. up sides. Put pan on baking sheet. Bake for 10 minutes at 350 degrees. Let cool on wire rack.
- In a food processor or blender, make a puree with raspberries, strain and remove seeds. Sprinkle the gelatin over cold water in a microwave safe bowl, let sit 1 minute. Put in the microwave for 40 seconds on high and stir. Let sit 1 minute or until the gelatin is dissolved completely.
- Mix cream cheese, vanilla and sugar until smooth in a little bowl. Slowly add in gelatin mixture and raspberry puree. Spread over the crust. Cover and chill for several hours or overnight.

Loosen carefully the sides from pan with a knife. Remove the pan's sides. Chill leftovers.

Nutrition Information
- Calories: 411 calories
- Total Carbohydrate: 42 g
- Cholesterol: 65 mg
- Total Fat: 24 g
- Fiber: 3 g
- Protein: 9 g
- Sodium: 397 mg

# Chocolate & Peanut Butter Mousse Cheesecake

"This simple cheesecake that doesn't need to bake is worth the wait. It consists of a layer of chocolate, peanut butter mousse and top with a delicious ganache. It will take some time to assemble the cheesecake but it's worth every effort."
Serving: 16 servings. | Prep: 50m | Ready in: 50m

Ingredients
- 1-1/2 cups chocolate wafer crumbs (about 24 wafers)
- 1/4 cup butter, melted
- MOUSSE LAYERS:
- 1-1/4 cups heavy whipping cream
- 5 oz. cream cheese, softened
- 2 tbsps. butter, softened
- 3/4 cup creamy peanut butter
- 1-1/4 cups confectioners' sugar
- 5 oz. bittersweet chocolate, chopped
- 1 milk chocolate candy bar (3-1/2 oz.), chopped
- 1/3 cup sugar
- 1/4 cup 2% milk
- 1 tsp. vanilla extract
- GANACHE:
- 6 oz. bittersweet chocolate, chopped
- 2/3 cup heavy whipping cream
- 1 tsp. vanilla extract

Direction

- Mix melted butter and wafer crumbs and spread the mixture on the bottom of the greased 9-inches springform pan.
- Whisk the cream in a bowl until it forms stiff peaks. In a separate big bowl, combine butter, peanut butter, and cream cheese until smooth. Stir in confectioners' sugar. Add half of the whipped cream. Pour the mixture all over the crust. Store it inside the refrigerator while making the following layer.
- In a small bowl, mix milk chocolates and bittersweet. Boil the milk and sugar in a small saucepan while stirring the mixture frequently until the sugar dissolves. Add the chocolates and whisk until smooth. Blend in vanilla. Set aside to room temperature and let it cool, stirring for some time. Add the leftover whipped cream. Spread the mixture evenly on top of the peanut butter layer. Store it inside the freezer for 2 hours until firm.
- Put the chocolate in a small bowl for the ganache. Boil the cream in a small saucepan. Add the chocolate and whisk the mixture until smooth. Stir in vanilla. Allow it to cool on room temperature, stirring occasionally until the ganache reached its thick spreading consistency. Spread the ganache over the cheesecake and store for another 1 hour until all set. Remove the rim from the pan.

Nutrition Information
- Calories: 467 calories
- Total Carbohydrate: 38 g
- Cholesterol: 62 mg
- Total Fat: 36 g
- Fiber: 2 g
- Protein: 7 g
- Sodium: 186 mg

# Chocolate Almond Cheesecake

""Everyone loves a good meal, but we all save room for dessert once this cheesecake is serve. It's rich chocolate flavor is so pleasing when we're craving something creamy and sweet.""
Serving: 12 servings. | Prep: 20m | Ready in: 01h05m

Ingredients
- 1-1/4 cups graham cracker crumbs
- 1-1/2 cups sugar, divided
- 1/2 cup plus 2 tbsps. baking cocoa, divided
- 1/4 cup butter, melted
- 2 packages (8 oz. each) cream cheese, softened
- 1 cup sour cream
- 1-1/2 tsps. almond extract, divided
- 3 large eggs, lightly beaten
- 1 cup heavy whipping cream
- 1/4 cup confectioners' sugar
- 1/4 cup sliced almonds, toasted

Direction
- In a small bowl, mix the butter, 2 tbsps. cocoa, 1/4 cup sugar and cracker crumbs. Then press on the bottom of the 9-inch springform pan. Let chill.
- In a big bowl, mix the leftover sugar, sour cream and cream cheese until it turns smooth. Mix in leftover cocoa and 1 tsp. extract. Put in eggs; whisk on low speed until mixed.

• Put in crust. Bake in the oven for 45 to 50 minutes at 350°F or until the middle is set. Transfer to a wire rack and cool for 10 minutes. Gently run a knife around the edges of the pan to loosen; cool for 1 more hour. Keep in the refrigerator overnight. Take off the sides of the pan.

• Beat cream in a big bowl until it starts to thicken. Put in leftover extract and confectioner's sugar; whisk until forms a stiff peak. Scatter evenly on cheesecake. Dust with almonds. Keep in refrigerator.

Nutrition Information
- Calories: 397 calories
- Total Carbohydrate: 39 g
- Cholesterol: 125 mg
- Total Fat: 25 g
- Fiber: 1 g
- Protein: 6 g
- Sodium: 181 mg

# Chocolate Banana Cheesecake

"A lightened cheesecake recipe for people who love cheesecakes and anything with bananas."
Serving: 16 servings. | Prep: 30m | Ready in: 60m

Ingredients
- 1 cup chocolate graham cracker crumbs (about 5 whole crackers)
- 1 tbsp. sugar
- 3 tbsps. butter, melted
- FILLING:
- 3 packages (8 oz. each) reduced-fat cream cheese
- 2/3 cup sugar
- 1 egg, lightly beaten
- 3 egg whites, lightly beaten
- 1/2 cup mashed ripe banana
- 1/2 cup miniature semisweet chocolate chips
- 1 tsp. vanilla extract
- 3 tbsps. baking cocoa
- 1 tbsp. canola oil

Direction
- To prepare the crust, combine cracker crumbs and sugar in a small bowl; mix in butter. Reserve 1/4 cup of the mixture to be used for the topping later. Coat a 9-in. springform pan with cooking spray and press the remaining crumb mixture onto the bottom. Place on a baking sheet and bake at 350 degrees for 7-9 minutes or until the crust has set. Set aside and let the crust cool on a wire rack.

- Combine cream cheese and sugar in a large bowl and keep beating until smooth. Pour in the egg and egg whites and beat on low speed just until incorporated. Gently add the chocolate chips, vanilla and banana. Divide the batter in half and pour the first half over the prepared crust.
- Combine cocoa and oil until blended; add the mixture into the remaining half of the batter. Put over the batter by tablespoonfuls in the pan, and gently spread the layer evenly. Sprinkle the reserved crumb mixture.
- Securely wrap a double thickness of heavy-duty foil, about 18 in. square, around the pan Place the wrapped pan in a large baking pan. Pour hot water in the larger pan up to 1-inch of the pan.
- Set oven to 350 degrees and bake cheesecake for 30-35 minutes or until center is set. Take out the pan from its water bath and transfer to a wire rack to cool for 10 minutes. Loosen the cheesecake from the pan by carefully running a knife around its edge. Cool for another 1 hour then refrigerate overnight. Take off the sides of the pan before slicing.

Nutrition Information
- Calories: 231 calories
- Total Carbohydrate: 20 g
- Cholesterol: 49 mg
- Total Fat: 15 g
- Fiber: 1 g
- Protein: 6 g
- Sodium: 246 mg

# Chocolate Berry Cheesecake

"A cheesecake featured with a fruity sauce making it great for celebrations."
Serving: 12-14 servings. | Prep: 20m | Ready in: 01h15m

Ingredients
- 1 cup crushed chocolate wafers (about 20 wafers)
- 2 tbsps. butter, melted
- 3 packages (8 oz. each) cream cheese, softened
- 1/2 cup sugar
- 2 cups (12 oz.) semisweet chocolate chips, melted and cooled
- 1/2 cup heavy whipping cream
- 1 tbsp. cornstarch
- 1 tsp. vanilla extract
- 4 eggs, lightly beaten
- RASPBERRY SAUCE:
- 2 tbsps. sugar
- 2 tsps. cornstarch
- 1/2 cup cranberry juice
- 1 package (12 oz.) frozen unsweetened raspberries, thawed

Direction
- Wrap heavy-duty foil double thick (about 18 inches square) securely around a greased 9-inch springform pan.
- Combine butter and wafer crumbs in a small bowl. Press mixture on bottom of the pan, set aside for later.
- Mix sugar and cream cheese until smooth in a big bowl. Add cream, chocolate, vanilla and cornstarch. Put the eggs in and use low speed on a mixer to just combine ingredients. Pour the

mixture in the crust. In a large baking pan, add an inch of hot water and place the springform pan in the baking pan.

• Bake for 55-60 minutes or until middle has just set and the top looks dull at 325 degrees. Get the springform from the baking pan and place on a wire rack to let cool for 10 minutes. Loosen the edges carefully with a knife and let cool for another hour. Chill overnight.

• Mix sugar, cranberry juice, and cornstarch in a saucepan until smooth. On medium heat, bring to boiling. Stir for a minute before taking from heat. Add in raspberries and let it completely cool. Present the cheesecake with the raspberry sauce and store leftovers in refrigerator.

# Chocolate Caramel Cheesecake

"A recipe that is sure to be a hit at every occasion. Decorate with chocolate sauce or caramel sauce."
Serving: 12 | Prep: 45m | Ready in: 1h30m

Ingredients
- 2 cups graham cracker crumbs
- 1/3 cup white sugar
- 1/2 cup butter, melted
- 30 individually wrapped caramels, unwrapped
- 3 tbsps. milk
- 3/4 cup chopped pecans
- 1 cup semisweet chocolate chips
- 3 (8 oz.) packages cream cheese, softened
- 3/4 cup white sugar
- 1 tsp. vanilla extract
- 3 eggs

Direction
- Mix graham cracker crumbs, melted butter and sugar in a medium bowl. Press mixture into the bottom and up sides 1 inch in a 9-in. springform pan. Spread melted caramel/ pecan mixture and refrigerate for 30 minutes.
- For caramel filling: mix caramels and milk in a saucepan. Stir and cook over low heat until smooth. Add in sliced pecans. Preheat the oven to 325°F or 165°C.
- Heat chocolate on top of double boiler and stir occasionally until smooth and melted. Take away from heat and to lukewarm let cool. Mix cream cheese, vanilla and sugar in a large bowl until smooth. Add in eggs one at a time. Fold 1/3 of filling in melted

chocolate. Pour chocolate mixture back in filling and beat until there are no more streaks. Spread mixture in the crust.

• Bake for 50 minutes or until the center is slightly set. Put a pan of water on the rack under the cheesecake while baking to avoid cracking. Open the door of the oven slightly to cool in the oven. Chill for 5 hours before serving.

Nutrition Information
• Calories: 624 calories;

• Total Carbohydrate: 59.8 g

• Cholesterol: 131 mg

• Total Fat: 41.1 g

• Protein: 9.3 g

• Sodium: 387 mg

# Chocolate Cheese Pie

""We got married in a casual outdoor ceremony. And our cake for the wedding contained of 30 yummy cheesecakes, including this simple but special one.""
Serving: 2 pies (8 servings each). | Prep: 35m | Ready in: 01h15m

Ingredients
- 3 cups graham cracker crumbs (about 48 squares)
- 1/2 cup sugar
- 2/3 cup butter, melted
- FILLING:
- 3 packages (8 oz. each) cream cheese, softened
- 1 cup sugar
- 5 eggs, lightly beaten
- 1 tbsp. vanilla extract
- 4 oz. German sweet chocolate, melted and cooled

Direction
- Mix sugar and cracker crumbs in a bowl; mix in butter. Split in half and press onto the bottom and up the sides of two ungreased 9-inch pie plates. Put in the refrigerator while making the filling.
- Beat cream cheese in a large bowl until fluffy. Gently add sugar, whisking until it becomes smooth. Put in eggs, then whisk on low speed just until blended. Add in vanilla. Take out 1-1/2 cups cheese mixture to a small bowl; fold in melted chocolate. Split remaining cream cheese mixture between pie crusts.
- To create the chain of hearts on each pie, put teaspoonfuls of chocolate filling, making 8 drops evenly spaced around outside

edges and 4 drops in the middle. Beginning in the middle of one outer drop, run a knife through the middle of each to connect the drops and make a circle of hearts and repeat with middle drops.

- Put in the oven and bake for 40-45 minutes at 350°F or until middle is nearly set. Put on wire racks for 1 hour to cool. Place in the refrigerator for at least 6 hours or overnight. Keep leftovers in the refrigerator.

Nutrition Information
- Calories: 313 calories
- Total Carbohydrate: 36 g
- Cholesterol: 102 mg
- Total Fat: 18 g
- Fiber: 0 g
- Protein: 5 g
- Sodium: 234 mg

# Chocolate Cheesecake

""A chocolate taste in this glossy and rich cheesecake is strengthen by the addition of coffee.""
Serving: 16 | Ready in: 1h35m

Ingredients
- Crust
- 4 oz. chocolate wafer, (18 wafers)
- 1 cup Grape-Nuts cereal
- 2 tbsps. unsweetened cocoa powder
- 2 tbsps. sugar
- 3 tbsps. canola oil
- 3 tbsps. water
- Filling
- 2 oz. semisweet chocolate
- 2 tbsps. instant coffee powder
- 1 tbsp. boiling water
- 2 16-oz. containers nonfat cottage cheese
- 1 8-oz. package low-fat cream cheese, at room temperature
- 1½ cups sugar
- 1 large egg
- 2 large egg whites
- 1 cup low-fat sour cream
- ¾ cup unsweetened cocoa powder
- 2 tbsps. cornstarch
- ⅛ tsp. salt
- 1 tsp. vanilla extract

Direction

- Prepare the oven by preheating to 325°F. Use nonstick cooking spray to coat a 9-inch springform pan.

- For crust: In a food processor, put the sugar, cocoa, Grape-Nuts and chocolate wafers; process until you have fine crumbs using an on/off motion. Put in water and oil; blend until the crumbs are moistened. Push down the crumb mixture into the bottom and about 1 1/2 inches up the sides of the prepared pan.

- For filling: Place chocolate and melt on the top of a double boiler over hot, but not boiling water or in a microwave oven at medium (50%) power. Allow to cool slightly.

- Melt instant coffee in the 1 tbsp. boiling water and reserve. Put in a strainer the cottage cheese lined with double thickness of cheesecloth. Gather the cheesecloth and squeeze out moisture from the cottage cheese. In a food processor, put the pressed cottage cheese solids and process until it turns smooth. Put in the melted coffee, melted chocolate, vanilla, salt, cornstarch, cocoa, sour cream, egg whites, egg, sugar and cream cheese; blend until becomes smooth. Place into the crust-lined pan.

- Put in the oven and bake for about 1 hour until firm around the edge but still slightly soft and shiny in the middle. Use a knife to run around the pan to loosen the edges. Allow to cool in the pan on a rack. Place in the refrigerator for at least 8 hours or for up to 2 days, covered, until well chilled. Take off the sides. To make cutting easier, dip a sharp knife in hot water and wipe dry prior to cutting each slice.

Nutrition Information
- Calories: 249 calories;
- Total Carbohydrate: 40 g
- Cholesterol: 25 mg
- Total Fat: 10 g

- Fiber: 3 g
- Protein: 5 g
- Sodium: 180 mg
- Sugar: 27 g
- Saturated Fat: 4 g

# Chocolate Cheesecake Bars

""Try this recipe if you don't have enough time to make a real cheesecake. Dough that is almond-flavored serves as both topping and crust for a soft chocolate filling.""
Serving: 4 dozen. | Prep: 15m | Ready in: 50m

Ingredients
- 1 cup butter, softened
- 1-1/2 cups sugar
- 2 large eggs
- 1/2 tsp. almond extract
- 3 cups all-purpose flour
- 1 tsp. baking powder
- 1/2 tsp. salt
- FILLING:
- 2 cups (12 oz.) semisweet chocolate chips
- 1 package (8 oz.) cream cheese
- 1 can (5 oz.) evaporated milk
- 1 cup chopped walnuts
- 1/2 tsp. almond extract

Direction
- Beat sugar and butter in a large bowl until fluffy and light. Mix in eggs, one at a time, whisking well after every addition. Mix in extract. Mix the salt, baking soda and flour; gently add to the creamed mixture and combine well. Then press half of the dough onto the bottom of a 13x9-inch baking pan that is greased. Reserve remaining dough for topping.

- To make filling, mix in a large saucepan combine the milk, cream cheese and chocolate chips; stir and cook over low heat until turns smooth. Separate from the heat; mix in extract and walnuts. Then spread over dough.
- And breaking off small pieces, put remaining dough over filling. Put in the oven and bake for 35-40 minutes at 375°F or until topping is golden brown. Fully cool on a wire rack. Slice into bars. Keep leftovers in the refrigerator.

Nutrition Information
- Calories: 160 calories
- Total Carbohydrate: 17 g
- Cholesterol: 25 mg
- Total Fat: 9 g
- Fiber: 1 g
- Protein: 3 g
- Sodium: 92 mg

# Chocolate Cheesecake Phyllo Tartlets

"This festive treat has a mousse-like mixture placed inside of a crispy phyllo shell. It's bite-size piece makes it a party favorite."
Serving: 2-1/2 dozen. | Prep: 15m | Ready in: 15m

Ingredients
- 1 package (8 oz.) cream cheese, softened
- 1/4 cup sugar
- 1/4 cup semisweet chocolate chips, melted
- 1/2 tsp. vanilla extract
- 2 packages (1.9 oz. each) frozen miniature phyllo tart shells
- Chocolate curls, optional

Direction
- Put together cream cheese, melted chocolate, sugar and vanilla in a small bowl and beat until smooth. Get a pastry or plastic bag and cut a little hole in the corner to insert a pastry tip with a #32 star. Place the cream cheese filling in the pastry bag and pipe into the tart shells. Adding some chocolate curls for decoration is optional. Place in the refrigerator till serving.

Nutrition Information
- Calories: 62 calories
- Total Carbohydrate: 5 g
- Cholesterol: 8 mg
- Total Fat: 4 g
- Fiber: 0 g
- Protein: 1 g
- Sodium: 32 mg

# Chocolate Cheesecake Squares

""This recipe is super rich, so small servings are pleasing. Perfect for parties since they don't require a plate and fork to eat.""
Serving: about 2 dozen. | Prep: 20m | Ready in: 40m

Ingredients
- 1 cup all-purpose flour
- 1/2 cup sugar
- 3 tbsps. baking cocoa
- 1 tsp. baking powder
- 1/4 tsp. salt
- 1/2 cup cold butter, cubed
- 1 large egg yolk
- 1 tsp. vanilla extract
- 1/2 cup finely chopped walnuts
- FILLING:
- 1 package (8 oz.) cream cheese, softened
- 1/3 cup sugar
- 1/2 cup sour cream
- 1 tbsp. all-purpose flour
- 2 tsps. grated orange zest
- 1/4 tsp. salt
- 1 large egg, lightly beaten
- 1 large egg white, lightly beaten
- 1/2 tsp. vanilla extract
- Chocolate sprinkles, optional

Direction

- Use foil to line a 9-inch square baking pan; then grease the foil and reserve. Mix in a large bowl the first five ingredients. Cut in butter until mixture is similar to fine crumbs. Mix in the walnuts, vanilla and egg yolk.
- Push down onto the bottom of prepared pan. Put in the oven and bake for 15 minutes at 325°F.
- Beat sugar and cream cheese in a small bowl until smooth. Mix in the salt, orange zest, flour and sour cream. Mix in the vanilla, egg white and egg on low speed just until mixed.
- Place filling over warm crust. Put in the oven and bake for 20-25 minutes or until middle is nearly set. Let it cool for 1 hour on a wire rack.
- Decorate with chocolate sprinkles if wished. Put in the refrigerator overnight. Lift out of the pan using foil; take off foil. Slice into 1-inch squares.

Nutrition Information
- Calories: 142 calories
- Total Carbohydrate: 12 g
- Cholesterol: 40 mg
- Total Fat: 10 g
- Fiber: 0 g
- Protein: 3 g
- Sodium: 135 mg

# Chocolate Cheesecake Triangles

""I love this delicious spin on traditional cheesecake. The chocolaty, creamy triangles are presented with a yummy raspberry sauce for a simple, eye-catching dessert.""
Serving: 16 servings. | Prep: 20m | Ready in: 55m

Ingredients
- 1-1/4 cups chocolate wafer crumbs
- 1/3 cup butter, melted
- 3 tbsps. plus 1/2 cup sugar, divided
- 2 packages (8 oz. each) cream cheese, softened
- 2 tbsps. all-purpose flour
- 1 can (5 oz.) evaporated milk
- 1 egg
- 2 tsps. vanilla extract
- 1 cup (6 oz.) semisweet chocolate chips, melted
- RASPBERRY SAUCE:
- 1 package (10 oz.) frozen sweetened raspberries, thawed and undrained
- 1 tsp. cornstarch
- 2 tbsps. cold water

Direction
- Use a heavy-duty foil to line the bottom and sides of a 9-inch square baking pan. Mix 3 tbsps. sugar. Butter and wafer crumbs in a small bowl; then press onto the bottom of prepared pan. Beat remaining sugar, flour and cream cheese in a large bowl. Mix in milk. Put in egg; whisk on low speed just until mixed. Mix in vanilla. Mix melted chocolate, and 3/4 cup cream cheese mixture in a separate bowl; reserve. Place remaining cream

cheese mixture over crust. Put spoonfuls of chocolate mixture on top; use a knife to cut through batter to swirl. Place in the oven and bake for 35-40 minutes at 325°F or until middle is almost set. Place on a wire rack and cool. Place in the refrigerator until chilled. In the meantime, to make sauce, put raspberries in a blender; then cover and blend well. Press through sieve over a small saucepan. Get rid of seeds. Mix water and cornstarch; mix into raspberry juice. Make it boil. Stir and cook for 2 minutes or until become thick. Place in the refrigerator until serving time. Lift cheesecake out of pan using foil; get rid of foil. Slice into 4 squares; slice each square diagonally into 4 triangles. Pair with sauce.

Nutrition Information
- Calories: 294 calories
- Total Carbohydrate: 29 g
- Cholesterol: 57 mg
- Total Fat: 19 g
- Fiber: 2 g
- Protein: 4 g
- Sodium: 176 mg

# Chocolate Cheesecakes

"This dessert is so creamy, sweet and rich in chocolate that would satisfy all the sweet tooth."
Serving: 2 dozen. | Prep: 15m | Ready in: 25m

Ingredients
- 24 miniature vanilla wafers or gingersnap cookies
- 1 package (8 oz.) reduced-fat cream cheese
- Sugar substitute equivalent to 1/2 cup sugar
- 1/2 cup semisweet chocolate chips, melted and cooled
- 1 tsp. vanilla extract
- 1 large egg, lightly beaten
- 1/3 cup heavy whipping cream
- 4 tsps. confectioners' sugar
- Chocolate curls, optional

Direction
- Lay the wafers, flat side down, in a paper-lined miniature muffin cups; put aside.
- Whisk sugar substitute and cream cheese in a small bowl until smooth. Stir in vanilla and chocolate chips. Add the egg and whisk at low speed just until blended. Fill the cups with at least 1 tbsp. of the mixture.
- Set the oven at 350°F and bake for 10-12 minutes until all set. Transfer into a wire rack to cool completely. Cover the cups and refrigerate for 60 minutes.
- Whisk the cream in a small bowl until its thick. Stir in confectioners' sugar and whisk until it forms stiff peaks. Spread the whipped cream mixture on top of the cheesecake and style it using chocolate curls if you want.

Nutrition Information
- Calories: 65 calories
- Total Carbohydrate: 5 g
- Cholesterol: 20 mg
- Total Fat: 5 g
- Fiber: 0 g
- Protein: 2 g
- Sodium: 50 mg

# Chocolate Cherry Cheesecake

"With only 15 minutes, now you can prepare and serve as much as 16 slices of Chocolate Cherry Cheesecake as an ideal dessert for a party."
Serving: 16 servings | Prep: 15m | Ready in: 1h45m

Ingredients
- 2 pkg. (21.4 oz. each) JELL-O No Bake Cherry Cheesecake Dessert
- 10 Tbsp. margarine, melted
- 1/4 cup sugar
- 2 Tbsp. water
- 3 cups cold milk
- 3 oz. BAKER'S Semi-Sweet Chocolate, melted, cooled

Direction
- 1. In a medium bowl, combine water, sugar, margarine and crust mixes with fork until crumbs are thoroughly moistened. In a 9" springform pan, press it firmly on bottom and 2" upside. On bottom of crust, spread contents of 1 fruit pouch.
- 2. In a medium mixing bowl, add milk. Add both Filling mixes and beat on low speed until blended, using mixer. Continue beating on medium speed for 3 minutes. The filling will be thick after the process. Take out 1 cup filling mixture; blend with melted chocolate. Add to leftover filling mixture and combine well. Ladle into crust. Put contents of leftover Fruit Pouch on top.
- 3. Chill in fridge until firm, or for at least 1 1/2 hours. Before serving, use a spatula or a small knife to run around side of pan to loosen crust then remove side of pan.

Nutrition Information
- Calories: 440
- Total Carbohydrate: 66 g
- Cholesterol: 5 mg
- Total Fat: 17 g
- Fiber: 2 g
- Protein: 5 g
- Sodium: 630 mg
- Sugar: 45 g
- Saturated Fat: 7 g

# Chocolate Chip Cheesecake

""My family well-loved recipe during a holiday from a version of the recipe on the cream cheese label. Very easy and super delicious!""

Serving: 8 | Prep: 15m | Ready in: 1h5m

Ingredients

- 1 individual package chocolate graham crackers, crushed
- 1/2 cup melted butter
- 2 tbsps. white sugar
- 2 (8 oz.) packages cream cheese, softened
- 1/2 cup brown sugar
- 2 eggs
- 1 egg yolk
- 1 tsp. vanilla extract
- 1 cup semisweet chocolate chips

Direction

- Prepare the oven by preheating to 350°F (175°C).Combine sugar, melted butter and cracker crumbs. Then press into the bottom and sides of a 9-inch pie plate. Place the crust in the refrigerator while preparing the filling.
- Mix brown sugar and cream cheese in a large bowl until smooth. Mix in the egg yolk and egg. Mix in vanilla. Fold in the chocolate chips. Place the filling into pie crust.
- Place in the preheated oven and bake for 50 minutes, or until filling is set.

Nutrition Information

- Calories: 567 calories;
- Total Carbohydrate: 46.1 g
- Cholesterol: 164 mg
- Total Fat: 41.1 g
- Protein: 8.5 g
- Sodium: 417 mg

# Chocolate Chip Cheesecake Dessert

Serving: 9 servings. | Prep: 20m | Ready in: 35m

Ingredients
- 1/2 cup graham cracker crumbs
- 2 tbsps. sugar
- 4 tsps. baking cocoa
- 3 tbsps. butter, melted
- 2/3 cup miniature semisweet chocolate chips, divided
- 1 package (8 oz.) cream cheese, softened
- 2/3 cup sweetened condensed milk
- 1 egg, lightly beaten
- 3/4 tsp. vanilla extract

Direction
- Mix cocoa, sugar and cracker crumbs in a small bowl; add butter and mix. On an 8-inch greased baking dish, compress the mixture onto the base. Place inside a 325°F oven and bake until color is golden brown, 10-12 minutes. Transfer to a wire to cool down.
- Dissolve 1/3 cup chocolate chips in a microwave; mix until consistency is smooth. Reserve. Whip cream cheese until fluffy in a little bowl; whip in slowly the melted chips and milk. Put in egg and vanilla; on a low speed, whip mixture until just mixed. Put in the crust; drizzle the remaining chips on top.
- Place inside the oven to bake at 325°F until it sets. Transfer to a wire rack to cool down, about 1 hour. Chill, covered, for 2 hours in refrigerator. Make square slices. Keep leftovers in refrigerator.

Nutrition Information
- Calories: 297 calories
- Total Carbohydrate: 28 g
- Cholesterol: 69 mg
- Total Fat: 19 g
- Fiber: 1 g
- Protein: 5 g
- Sodium: 179 mg

# Chocolate Chip Cherry Cheesecake

"The flavor combination of this cheesecake has been a huge success, and this dessert came about from creating and modifying different recipes."

Serving: 6 servings. | Prep: 15m | Ready in: 45m

Ingredients
- 1 jar (12 oz.) maraschino cherries
- 2 packages (8 oz. each) cream cheese, softened
- 1/2 cup sugar
- 2 eggs, lightly beaten
- 1/2 cup miniature semisweet chocolate chips
- 1 chocolate cookie crust (9 inches)
- 6 chocolate-covered cherries

Direction
- Reserve 2 tsps. juice from draining the maraschino cherries. Cut the cherries into quarters and set aside.
- Beat the sugar, cream cheese and reserved cherry juice in a small bowl until smooth. Put the eggs in and beat until just combined. Fold the reserved cherries and chocolate chips into the mixture.
- Set oven to 350 degrees. Pour prepared mixture into the crust and bake until the center is almost set or for 30 to 35 minutes. Remove from the oven and let it cool on a wire rack. Chill cheesecake in the refrigerator. Garnish with chocolate-covered cherries to serve.

Nutrition Information
- Calories: 682 calories

- Total Carbohydrate: 77 g
- Cholesterol: 154 mg
- Total Fat: 41 g
- Fiber: 2 g
- Protein: 10 g
- Sodium: 384 mg

# Chocolate Chip Cookie Cheesecake

""Our daughter surprised us with her first cooking talents when she prepares this cheesecake at 13 years of age. Everyone think this dessert was created by a gourmet baker because of its different cookie crumb crust and extra-creamy filling!""
Serving: 12-14 servings. | Prep: 20m | Ready in: 01h25m

Ingredients
- 2 cups chocolate chip cookie crumbs (about 28 cookies)
- 3 tbsps. sugar
- 5 tbsps. butter, melted
- FILLING:
- 5 packages (8 oz. each) cream cheese, softened
- 1-1/4 cup sugar
- 3 tbsps. all-purpose flour
- 5 large eggs, lightly beaten
- 2 large egg yolks, lightly beaten
- 1/4 cup sour cream
- 1/2 tsp. vanilla extract
- 1 cup miniature semisweet chocolate chips
- 1 tsp. grated orange zest
- TOPPING:
- 1 cup sour cream
- 2 tbsps. sugar
- 1 tsp. vanilla extract
- 1 tbsp. chocolate chip cookie crumbs

Direction

- Mix in a large bowl the sugar and cookie crumbs; mix in butter; then press onto the bottom and 2-inch up the sides of a greased 9-inch springform pan; reserve.

- Beat flour, sugar and cream cheese in a separate bowl until it turns smooth. Put in egg yolks and eggs; whisk on low speed just until mixed. Mix in vanilla and sour cream. Add in chocolate chips and orange zest and fold. Put into crust. Move the pan to a baking sheet.

- Place in the oven and bake for 65-75 minutes at 325°F or until the middle is nearly set. Take out from the oven; allow to stand for 5 minutes.

- Mix in a small bowl the vanilla, sugar and sour cream; then spread over filling. Put it back to the oven for 8 minutes. Place on a wire rack and cool for 10 minutes.

- Gently run a knife around the edge of the pan to loosen. Cool for 1 more hour. Keep in the refrigerator for overnight. Decorate with cookie crumbs.

Nutrition Information
- Calories: 432 calories
- Total Carbohydrate: 47 g
- Cholesterol: 149 mg
- Total Fat: 25 g
- Fiber: 1 g
- Protein: 7 g
- Sodium: 201 mg

# Chocolate Chip Cookie Dough Cheesecake

""You will surely love this recipe if you love chocolate chip cookie dough straight out of the batter bowl or in ice cream! Small portion goes a long way! So worth the effort!""
Serving: 12 | Prep: 30m | Ready in: 5h20m

Ingredients
- Crust:
- 1 1/2 cups finely crushed chocolate wafer cookies
- 2 tbsps. white sugar
- 1/4 cup melted butter
- Cake:
- 2 (8 oz.) packages cream cheese, cut into chunks
- 3/4 cup white sugar
- 2 tbsps. white sugar
- 1 cup sour cream
- 3 large eggs
- 1 tsp. vanilla extract
- Cookie Dough:
- 1/4 cup butter, softened
- 1/4 cup firmly packed brown sugar
- 1/4 cup white sugar
- 2 tbsps. water
- 1 tsp. vanilla extract
- 1 cup semisweet chocolate chips
- 1/2 cup all-purpose flour
- Topping:
- 1 cup sour cream

- 2 tsps. white sugar
- 1 tsp. vanilla extract

Direction
- Preheat oven to 350 degrees F (175°C).
- In a bowl, combine melted butter, 2 tbsps. white sugar, and chocolate wafer cookie crumbs. Push firmly into the bottom and 1/2-inch up the sides of a 9-inch springform pan.
- Place crust in the preheated oven and bake for about 8 minutes until set.
- In a bowl, beat cream cheese and 3/4 cup plus 2 tbsps. white sugar until become creamy. Put in 1 tsp. vanilla extract, eggs and 1 cup sour cream; whisk until batter turn smooth. Place batter over crust into springform pan. Whisk in a bowl the 1/4 cup white sugar, brown sugar and 1/4 cup batter. Mix in 1 tsp. vanilla extract and water into brown sugar mixture. Put in flour and chocolate chips; mix until cookie dough is mixed well. Then drop cookie dough in 2 tbsp. portions equally over the top of the cheesecake, pressing dough beneath the surface of the batter.
- Place in the preheated oven and bake for about 40 minutes until cheesecake is almost fully set and jiggles slightly in middle when shaken.
- In a bowl, mix 1 tsp. vanilla, 2 tsps. white sugar, and 1 cup sour cream until turns smooth. Place sour cream mixture over hot cheesecake and spread. Let cake cool at a room temperature and place in the refrigerator for at least 4 hours until cold.

Nutrition Information
- Calories: 549 calories;
- Total Carbohydrate: 51.8 g
- Cholesterol: 125 mg
- Total Fat: 36.2 g

- Protein: 7.7 g
- Sodium: 287 mg

# Chocolate Chip Cookie Tart

""Suitable refrigerated cookie dough is a delicious crust for a creamy peanut butter filling in this luscious dessert. So easy to make and we love it.""

Serving: 10-12 servings. | Prep: 15m | Ready in: 35m

Ingredients
- 1 tube (18 oz.) refrigerated chocolate chip cookie dough
- 1 package (8 oz.) cream cheese, softened
- 2 tbsps. creamy peanut butter
- 1 tbsp. butter, softened
- 2 cups confectioners' sugar
- 1/4 cup milk chocolate chips, melted and cooled

Direction
- Onto the bottom of an ungreased 9-inch springform pan, press cookie dough. Place in the oven and bake for 20-24 minutes at 350°F or until golden brown in color. Put on a wire rack to cool.
- Whisk butter, peanut butter and cream cheese in a small bowl until it turns smooth. Mix in confectioner's sugar. Put the crust on a serving plate. Put cream cheese mixture over the crust and spread to within 1/2-inch of the edge. Then drizzle with melted chocolate. Keep in the refrigerator for 1 hour or until set.

Nutrition Information
- Calories: 374 calories
- Total Carbohydrate: 49 g
- Cholesterol: 34 mg
- Total Fat: 19 g

- Fiber: 1 g
- Protein: 4 g
- Sodium: 170 mg

# Chocolate Cookie Cheesecake

"Recipe for a truly decadent and addictive dessert."
Serving: 14 | Prep: 30m | Ready in: 11h

Ingredients
- 2 cups chocolate sandwich cookie crumbs
- 2 tbsps. butter, melted
- 1/4 cup packed brown sugar
- 1 tsp. ground cinnamon
- 2 lbs. cream cheese, softened
- 1 1/4 cups white sugar
- 1/3 cup heavy whipping cream
- 2 tbsps. all-purpose flour
- 1 tsp. vanilla extract
- 4 eggs
- 1 1/2 cups chocolate sandwich cookie crumbs
- 16 oz. sour cream
- 1/4 cup white sugar
- 1 tsp. vanilla extract
- 1 cup heavy whipping cream
- 1 1/2 cups semisweet chocolate chips
- 1 tsp. vanilla extract

Direction
- In a medium bowl, combine these ingredients together - 2 cups cookie crumbs, cinnamon, melted butter and brown sugar. Use a 10-inch springform pan, press the mixture firmly onto the

bottom and 1 inch up the sides. Bake for 5 minutes at 350 degrees Fahrenheit or 175 degrees Celsius. Keep aside.

• Meanwhile, in a large bowl, beat cream cheese until texture becomes smooth. Slowly mix in 1 1/4 cups sugar, 1/3 cup whipping cream, flour, and 1 tsp. vanilla. Drop eggs one at a time, beat the mixture well after each egg has been added. Measure 1/3 of the batter and pour into the prepared pan. Put 1 1/2 cups cookie pieces on top then pour in remaining batter.

• Bake for 45 minutes at 350 degrees Fahrenheit or 175 degrees Celsius. Remove cake from the oven. Combine 1/4 cup sugar, sour cream and 1 tsp. vanilla; spread this evenly on top of the cheesecake. Return to the oven and continue baking for another 7 minutes. Turn off the oven and leave the cake in the oven for 30 minutes. Transfer cheesecake to a wire rack to let it cool completely.

• Combine chocolate chips and 1 cup whipping cream in a saucepan and stir over low heat until chocolate is fully melted; stir in 1 tsp vanilla. Pour over cheesecake while still warm. Keep cheesecake in the refrigerator for at least 8 hours. Before serving, take the cheesecake out of the fridge and let it sit for about 1/2 hour to 1 hour. Remove ring from springform pan, decorate and serve.

Nutrition Information
• Calories: 753 calories;
• Total Carbohydrate: 62.9 g
• Cholesterol: 174 mg
• Total Fat: 52 g
• Protein: 11.2 g
• Sodium: 348 mg

# Chocolate Cran-Raspberry Cheesecake Bars

"Baking cocoa, raspberries, and cranberries blend well to bring this dish into another level. Make a bunch of this cheesecake dish since it's a hit on any substantial social events."
Serving: 2 dozen. | Prep: 25m | Ready in: 01h10m

Ingredients
- 1-3/4 cups sugar, divided
- 3 tbsps. cornstarch
- 3 cups fresh or frozen cranberries, thawed
- 1 cup fresh or frozen raspberries, thawed
- 1/2 cup cranberry juice
- 2 cups crushed vanilla wafers (about 60 wafers)
- 5 tbsps. butter, melted
- 3 tbsps. baking cocoa
- 3 packages (8 oz. each) cream cheese, softened
- 1 cup (8 oz.) sour cream
- 3/4 cup egg substitute
- 3/4 cup semisweet chocolate chips, melted
- 1-1/2 tsps. vanilla extract
- Additional melted semisweet chocolate and fresh raspberries, optional

Direction
- Mix cornstarch and a 3/4 cup of sugar in a big saucepan. Add the cranberry juice and berries. Cook the mixture on moderate heat, stirring it constantly until the mixture boils. Remove the mixture from the heat and allow it to cool.

- In a big bowl, mix cocoa, butter, and wafer crumbs. Pour the mixture into the greased 13x9-inches baking dish. Spread the berry mixture all over the crust.
- Whisk sour cream, sugar, and cream cheese in a separate bowl until smooth. Stir in egg substitute and whisk at low speed until just incorporated. Mix in vanilla and melted chocolate. Pour the mixture on top of the berry mixture.
- Set the oven to 325°F and bake the cheesecake for 45-55 minutes until the center is fixed. Transfer it onto a wire rack and allow it to cool for 60 minutes. Cover the dish and store it inside the fridge for 8 hours up to overnight. You can garnish it with melted chocolate and raspberries on top if you want. Serve.

Nutrition Information
- Calories: 283 calories
- Total Carbohydrate: 30 g
- Cholesterol: 46 mg
- Total Fat: 17 g
- Fiber: 2 g
- Protein: 4 g
- Sodium: 150 mg

# Chocolate Cranberry Cheesecake

""Chocolate cranberry flavored cheesecake decorated by topping with a thick chocolate glaze.""
Serving: 10-12 servings. | Prep: 15m | Ready in: 45m

Ingredients
- 1-1/3 cups chocolate wafer crumbs
- 1/4 cup sugar
- 1/4 cup butter, melted
- FILLING:
- 2 packages (8 oz. each) cream cheese, softened
- 1/2 cup sugar
- 1 tbsp. cornstarch
- 2 eggs, lightly beaten
- 3/4 cup sour cream
- 1 cup whole-berry cranberry sauce
- 1/4 cup hot fudge ice cream topping, warmed

Direction
- Mix butter, sugar and wafer crumbs in a small bowl. In a greased 9-inch springform pan, place mixture and press 1 inch up each side and on bottom. Reserve.

- Beat cornstarch, cream cheese, and sugar in a big bowl until consistency is smooth. Put in eggs; on low speed mix until ingredients are just mixed. Add sour scream. Mix cranberry sauce in by folding. Put in crust. On a baking sheet, place the pan.

- Put inside the oven and bake for 30-35 minutes at 325°F or until it has nearly set. Transfer to a wire rack and let to cool down for 10 minutes. Loosen the cake by running a knife cautiously around the pan's edges; allow cooling down for 1 hour more. Put in refrigerator for a night.

• Use fudge topping to drizzle on the plates; place cheesecake on top. Keep leftovers in refrigerator.

Nutrition Information
• Calories: 302 calories
• Total Carbohydrate: 36 g
• Cholesterol: 77 mg
• Total Fat: 16 g
• Fiber: 1 g
• Protein: 4 g
• Sodium: 198 mg

# Chocolate Glazed Cheesecake

"This triple-layer cheesecake is sure to hit the spot of dessert lovers. I'm always requested to make this timeless dessert for years!"

Serving: 12 servings. | Prep: 40m | Ready in: 01h35m

Ingredients
- 1 package (9 oz.) chocolate wafer cookies, crushed
- 3/4 cup sugar, divided
- 1/2 cup butter, melted
- 2 packages (8 oz. each) plus 3 oz. cream cheese, softened, divided
- 3 large eggs, divided use
- 1 tsp. vanilla extract, divided
- 2 oz. semisweet chocolate, melted and cooled
- 1-1/3 cups sour cream, divided
- 1/3 cup packed dark brown sugar
- 1 tbsp. all-purpose flour
- 1/4 cup chopped pecans
- 1/4 tsp. almond extract
- CHOCOLATE GLAZE:
- 3 oz. semisweet chocolate
- 2 tbsps. butter
- 1/3 cup sifted confectioners' sugar
- 1 tbsp. water
- 1/2 tsp. vanilla extract
- Chopped pecans, optional

Direction
- Using around 18-inch square heavy-duty foil wrap a 9-inch ungreased springform pan. Combine cookie crumbs, 1/4 cup sugar and butter; press onto the bottom of the pan and up to the sides for about 2 inches. Set aside.
- In a large bowl, beat one package of cream cheese (8oz) and 1/4 cup of sugar until light. Add one egg and 1/4 tsp. vanilla extract. Mix well. Then stir in the chocolate and 1/3 cup sour cream. Pour onto the crust.
- On a separate bowl, cream together 1 package of cream cheese (8oz), brown sugar and flour until fully. Incorporate one egg and 1/2 tsp. vanilla. Add Pecans. Stir well. Pour on top of the chocolate layer.
- Beat the remaining cream cheese and sugar on a separate bowl until fluffy. Mix in the remaining egg, sour cream, and vanilla. Add almond extract. Carefully pour over the pecan layer.
- Bake for 55 minutes at 325°F or until the center is set to touch. Turn off the open and leave the cheesecake inside for 30 minutes; partway on cooling leave the oven door ajar and cool for 30 minutes more.
- Remove from the oven; cool. Refrigerate for at least 8 hours.
- To make the glaze, melt the chocolate and butter. Stir in water, confectioners' sugar and vanilla until smooth. Remove the cheesecake from the pan and pour the warm glaze on top. Serve and garnish with pecans.

Nutrition Information
- Calories: 467 calories
- Total Carbohydrate: 42 g
- Cholesterol: 125 mg
- Total Fat: 31 g
- Fiber: 1 g

- Protein: 7 g
- Sodium: 328 mg

# Chocolate Macadamia Cheesecake

""Prepare this recipe when one of my workmates turned 50. It was gone quickly and no crumb left on the platter!""
Serving: 12 servings. | Prep: 35m | Ready in: 01h30m

Ingredients
- 1-1/4 cups chocolate wafer crumbs (about 25 wafers)
- 1/4 cup ground macadamia nuts
- 2 tbsps. sugar
- 3 tbsps. butter, melted
- 1/8 tsp. almond extract
- FILLING:
- 8 oz. white baking chocolate, chopped
- 4 packages (8 oz. each) cream cheese, softened
- 3/4 cup sugar
- 3 tbsps. all-purpose flour
- 1 tsp. vanilla extract
- 5 eggs
- 1/3 cup milk chocolate chips
- TOPPING:
- 8 oz. semisweet chocolate, chopped
- 7 tbsps. heavy whipping cream
- White chocolate shavings and chopped macadamia nuts

Direction
- Mix the sugar, nuts, and wafer crumbs in a small bowl; mix in almonds extract and butter. Then press on the bottom of a 10-inch springform pan that is greased then press. Place in the oven

and bake for 10 minutes at 350°F. Place on a wire rack to cool. Lower heat to 325°F.

- Melt white chocolate in a microwave at 70% power for a minute; stir. Microwave for more 10-20 second intervals, whisking until it becomes smooth. Let cool. In a large bowl, mix the vanilla, flour, sugar and cream cheese until well combined. Put in eggs; whisk on low speed just until mixed. Take 1 cup and reserve. Mix melted white chocolate into leftover cream cheese mixture; whisk just until mixed. Put over crust.
- Melt chocolate chips in a microwave; mix until smooth. Slightly cool. Mix in leftover cream cheese mixture; then drop by spoonfuls on filling. Use a knife to slice through filling to swirl the chocolate mixture.
- Transfer pan on a baking sheet. Place in the oven and bake for 55-60 minutes at 325°F or until center is just set. Transfer to a wire rack and cool for 10 minutes. Cautiously run a knife around edge of pan to loosen. Cool for 1 more hour.
- Melt semisweet chocolate with cream in a saucepan on low heat; mix until turns smooth. Slightly cool. Pour over cheesecake and spread. Put on a wire rack to cool for 10 minutes. Keep in the refrigerator for four hours or overnight.
- Store leftovers in the refrigerator. Decorate with macadamia nuts and chocolate shavings.

# Chocolate Malt Cheesecake

"Make a good crust from graham cracker crumbs instead of the pretzel crumbs. Chocolate malt and cheesecake lovers will surely crave this."

Serving: 14 servings. | Prep: 25m | Ready in: 01h25m

Ingredients
- 1 cup graham cracker crumbs (about 16 squares)
- 1/4 cup sugar
- 1/3 cup butter, melted
- FILLING:
- 3 packages (8 oz. each) cream cheese, softened
- 1 can (14 oz.) sweetened condensed milk
- 3/4 cup chocolate malt powder
- 4 large eggs, lightly beaten
- 1 cup semisweet chocolate chips, melted and cooled
- 1 tsp. vanilla extract
- Confectioners' sugar and chocolate curls, optional

Direction
- Mix sugar together with butter and cracker crumbs. Grease a 9-inch springform pan and press the mixture onto its bottom.
- Beat until smooth the milk and cream cheese in a big bowl. Stir in malt powder well. Add the eggs and beat it on low speed until the ingredients are just combined. Mix in vanilla and the melted chocolate until combined; pour it in the crust. Transfer the pan to a baking tray.
- Let it bake at 325°F until the center is nearly set, 60-65 minutes. Let it cool on a wire rack, 10 minutes. Loosen from pan

by running a knife carefully around the edges. Let it cool an hour; then put inside the refrigerator overnight.

• Remove pan's sides. If you want, you can decorate it with chocolate curls and confectioners' sugar. Be sure to refrigerate any leftovers.

Nutrition Information
• Calories: 369 calories

• Total Carbohydrate: 47 g

• Cholesterol: 101 mg

• Total Fat: 19 g

• Fiber: 1 g

• Protein: 7 g

• Sodium: 291 mg

# Chocolate Mousse Cheesecake

""Prepare the day before desired: this cake gets better with time. Created in a pressure cooker. Decorate with whipped cream or confectioner's sugar and sliced strawberries if desired.""

Serving: 10 | Prep: 15m | Ready in: 1day1h15m

Ingredients
- 1/2 cup chocolate cookie crumbs
- 1 pinch ground cinnamon
- 8 (1 oz.) squares semisweet chocolate
- 1 tbsp. butter
- 2 (8 oz.) packages cream cheese, softened
- 1 cup heavy whipping cream
- 1 tsp. vanilla extract
- 2/3 cup white sugar
- 2 eggs, beaten
- 1 1/2 tbsps. unsweetened cocoa powder
- 1 1/2 cups water

Direction
- Prepare a greased 8-inch springform pan that will fit inside the pressure cooker. Combine cinnamon and chocolate wafer crumbs. Dust the crumb mixture on the bottom of springform pan, pushing gently to make the crust.
- Then melt butter and chocolate together and reserve.
- Process cream cheese until turn smooth using an electric mixer or food processor. Put in the chocolate mixture, and blend until mixture is well-combined and uniformly colored. Mix in the eggs, sugar, vanilla extract and cream. Blend well. Strain cocoa over

batter, and blend or mix on low speed until cocoa is well combined. Place mixture over crumbs in pan. Use a piece of waxed paper to cover the cake. Use aluminum foil to wrap the entire pan.

- Put water to pressure cooker. Put pan on the trivet in pressure cooker. Secure the cooker and make it up to 15 lbs. (high) pressure. Lower the heat to keep the pressure. Cook for 45-50 minutes. Remove cooker from heat and let the pressure drop on its own. Take the cheesecake from cooker, and allow to cool at a room temperature in pan on a wire rack.
- Take cheesecake from pan, and place in the refrigerator for 8 hours prior to serving.

Nutrition Information
- Calories: 454 calories;
- Total Carbohydrate: 32.7 g
- Cholesterol: 122 mg
- Total Fat: 34.7 g
- Protein: 7.3 g
- Sodium: 197 mg

# Chocolate Peanut Butter Cheesecake

""Everyone says "aah" and "ooh" all the time whenever I bring this enticing cheesecake after holiday dinners! Packed with cream cheese and peanut butter and drizzle with chocolate in a fudge crust, it's a showstopper.""
Serving: 12 servings. | Prep: 40m | Ready in: 01h45m

Ingredients
- BROWNIE CRUST:
- 1/4 cup butter, cubed
- 3 oz. unsweetened chocolate
- 1 cup packed brown sugar
- 2 large eggs
- 1-1/2 tsps. vanilla extract
- 2/3 cup all-purpose flour
- 1/8 tsp. baking powder
- 1 oz. semisweet chocolate, chopped
- FILLING:
- 1 jar (12 oz.) creamy peanut butter
- 11 oz. cream cheese, softened
- 1 cup packed brown sugar
- 3 large eggs
- 1/2 cup sour cream
- TOPPING:
- 3/4 cup sour cream
- 2 tsps. sugar
- Salted peanuts and melted semisweet chocolate, optional

Direction
- Dissolve unsweetened chocolate and butter in a microwave; whisk until smooth. Reserve. Beat eggs and brown sugar in a large bowl for about 4 minutes, until fluffy and light. Mix in vanilla and chocolate mixture. Combine baking powder and flour; gently add to batter and blend well. Mix in chopped chocolate.
- Spread 1 cup into a 9-inch springform pan that is greased. Place remaining batter in the refrigerator, covered. Put the pan on baking sheet. Place in the oven and bake for 17-19 minutes at 350°F or until a toothpick pricked in the middle comes out clean. Place on a wire rack and cool for 5 minutes; put in the freezer for 15 minutes.
- To make filling, beat brown sugar, cream cheese and peanut butter in a large bowl until smooth. Put in sour cream and eggs; whisk on low speed just until mixed. Spread remaining brownie batter about 1-1/2 inch high around sides of pan, securing to baked crust.
- Place filling into middle. Put in the oven and bake for 45 minutes at 350°F or until middle is just set.
- To make topping, mix sugar and sour cream; then spread over filling to within 3/4 inch of edges. Put the cheesecake back to the oven; switch off the oven and allow to stand for 5 minutes. Place on a wire rack and let cool for 10 minutes. Cautiously run a knife around pan to loosen; cool for 1 more hour. Keep for overnight in the refrigerator. Put peanuts on top and drizzle with melted chocolate if wished. Keep leftovers in the refrigerator.

Nutrition Information
- Calories: 564 calories
- Total Carbohydrate: 51 g
- Cholesterol: 144 mg
- Total Fat: 36 g

- Fiber: 2 g
- Protein: 14 g
- Sodium: 306 mg

# Chocolate Pecan Cheesecake

"Very easy to fix pie dessert. The combination of caramel and chocolate makes this creamy cheesecake, one magnificent dessert!"

Serving: 8 servings. | Prep: 25m | Ready in: 25m

Ingredients
- 25 caramels
- 1/4 cup evaporated milk
- 3/4 cup chopped pecans, divided
- 1 chocolate crumb crust (9 inches)
- 2 packages (3 oz. each) cream cheese, softened
- 1/2 cup sour cream
- 1-1/4 cups cold 2% milk
- 1 package (3.9 oz.) instant chocolate pudding mix
- 1/2 cup hot fudge ice cream topping, warmed

Direction

- Combine evaporated milk and caramels in a small saucepan. Cook and stir over medium low heat until smooth. Add 1/2 cup pecans. Pour mixture into crust and chill for 15 minutes.

- In a large bowl, beat sour cream and cream cheese until smooth. Meanwhile, using another small bowl, beat pudding mix and milk for 2 minutes. Add this together with cream cheese mixture, blend well until all ingredients have been incorporated. Spread over the caramel mixture Refrigerate for at least 30 minutes. To serve, garnish with the remaining pecans and drizzle hot fudge on top.

Nutrition Information

- Calories: 548 calories
- Total Carbohydrate: 68 g
- Cholesterol: 41 mg
- Total Fat: 28 g
- Fiber: 3 g
- Protein: 9 g
- Sodium: 503 mg

# Chocolate Raspberry Cheesecake

""A perfect recipe ending to any meal! Treat everyone with this creamy and sweet dessert.""

Serving: 8 | Prep: 15m | Ready in: 50m

Ingredients
- 2 (3 oz.) packages cream cheese, softened
- 1 (14 oz.) can sweetened condensed milk
- 1 egg
- 3 tbsps. ReaLemon® lemon juice from concentrate
- 1 tsp. vanilla extract
- 1 cup fresh or frozen raspberries
- 1 (6 oz.) ready-made graham cracker crumb crust
- 2 oz. semisweet chocolate
- 1/4 cup whipping cream

Direction
- Prepare the oven by preheating to 350°F. Beat cream cheese with mixer until fluffy. Add in sweetened condensed milk and gently beat in until smooth. Put in vanilla, ReaLemon® and egg and combine well. Then press firmly the raspberries into the bottom of the crust, setting aside a few whole berries for decoration. Gradually pour cream cheese mixture over fruit. Place in the preheated oven and bake for 30-35 minutes or until middle is nearly set. Let it cool.
- Chocolate glaze: Melt semisweet chocolate with whipping cream in a small saucepan over low heat. Stir until it turns smooth and thickened. Separate from heat. Then glaze over cheesecake. Chill. Decorate as wished.

Nutrition Information
- Calories: 415 calories;
- Total Carbohydrate: 47.2 g
- Cholesterol: 73 mg
- Total Fat: 22.7 g
- Protein: 8 g
- Sodium: 258 mg

# Chocolate Sandwich Cookie Cheesecake

"This delicious and also easy-making Chocolate Sandwich Cookie Cheesecake will make you say "Woah!""
Serving: 16 servings | Prep: 20m | Ready in: 6h30m

Ingredients
- 36  Reduced Fat OREO Cookies , divided
- 1/4 cup  butter , melted
- 4 pkg. (8 oz. each) PHILADELPHIA Neufchatel Cheese , softened
- 1 cup  sugar
- 1 tsp.  vanilla
- 1 cup  BREAKSTONE'S Reduced Fat or KNUDSEN Light Sour Cream
- 4  egg s

Direction
- 1. Break 28 cookies to create fine crumbs and combine with butter. Turn it on bottom of 9" springform pan, press and spread evenly.
- 2. In a large bowl, use mixer to beat vanilla, sugar and Neufchatel until well blended. Add in sour cream and mix thoroughly. One at a time, add eggs, beating after each addition until blended. Crush or chop leftover cookies. Slowly stir 1 1/2 cups of the chopped cookies into batter. Spill on crust and dredge in leftover chopped cookies.
- 3. Bake till it's mostly set in the middle, or for 70 minutes. Loosen cake by running knife around rim of pan. Let it cool before removing rim. Chill in fridge for 4 hours.

Nutrition Information

- Calories: 360
- Total Carbohydrate: 35 g
- Cholesterol: 95 mg
- Total Fat: 22 g
- Fiber: 1 g
- Protein: 8 g
- Sodium: 440 mg
- Sugar: 25 g
- Saturated Fat: 12 g

# Chocolate Swirl Cheesecake

"Perfect combination of chocolate and orange makes a delicious and creamy cheesecake."
Serving: 12-16 servings. | Prep: 25m | Ready in: 01h40m

Ingredients
- 1/3 cup graham cracker crumbs
- 4 packages (8 oz. each) cream cheese, softened
- 1-1/3 cups sugar
- 4 large eggs, lightly beaten
- 2 tbsps. orange juice
- 2 tsps. grated orange zest
- 3 oz. semisweet chocolate, melted
- Whipped cream, optional

Direction
- Lightly greased a 9-inch springform pan and place in it an 18 inch double-thick square of heavy-duty foil. Wrap foil it tightly around the pan. Put crumbs on the sides and bottom of the pan. Put it aside.
- Whisk sugar and cream cheese in a big bowl and mix well until it turns smooth. On low speed, beat the eggs until just combined. Mix in the zest and orange juice. Reserve 3/4 cup of mixture; add the remaining into the prepared pan.
- Mix in chocolates to the reserved mixture. By spoonful drop onto the filling. Cut through batter and swirl the chocolate by using a knife.
- Place the pan on a larger baking pan and add one inch of hot water to the baking pan making a water bath. Let it bake at

350°F until it looks dull and the center has just set, 75 to 80 minutes.

• Remove it from the water bath and let it cool 10 minutes on a wire rack. Gently loosen from pan by running a knife around edges. Set aside for an hour; store in refrigerator overnight. If you like, you can serve it with whipped cream.

Nutrition Information
• Calories: 315 calories
• Total Carbohydrate: 23 g
• Cholesterol: 115 mg
• Total Fat: 23 g
• Fiber: 0 g
• Protein: 6 g
• Sodium: 196 mg

# Chocolate Swirled Cheesecake

"Serve this enticing and delightful cheesecake in your family gatherings, they will love it."
Serving: 12 servings. | Prep: 30m | Ready in: 01h10m

Ingredients
- 2 cups 2% cottage cheese
- 1 cup crushed chocolate wafers (about 16 wafers)
- 1 package (8 oz.) reduced-fat cream cheese, cubed
- 1/2 cup sugar
- Dash salt
- 1 tbsp. vanilla extract
- 2 large eggs, lightly beaten
- 1 large egg white
- 2 oz. bittersweet chocolate, melted and cooled
- Fresh raspberries, optional

Direction
- Put a strainer on the bowl and line it with a coffee filter or 4 layers of cheesecloth. Put the cottage cheese over the strainer and place it inside the refrigerator, covered, for 60 minutes. Place the 9-inches springform pan over an 18-inch double thick and heavy-duty square shaped foil. Wrap the foil tightly around the pan. Use cooking spray to coat the pan. Place the crushed wafers into the pan, pressing it into its bottom and an inch up the sides.

- Set the oven to 350°F for preheating. Blend the drained cottage cheese in a food processor until smooth. Mix in sugar, salt, and cream cheese until well-blended. Transfer the mixture into a bowl and beat in vanilla, egg white, and eggs. Reserve 1 cup of the batter and place it in a bowl with melted chocolate.

• Pour the batter over the crust and coat it with spoonful of chocolate batter. Use a knife to swirl the batter. Pour boiling water into a bigger baking pan, about 1-inch of the bigger pan, and submerge the springform pan.

• Place it inside the preheated oven and bake for 40 minutes until the center is fixed and the top looks dull. Turn off the oven and open its door to allow the cheesecake to cool for 30 minutes.

• Get the springform pan from the water bath and remove its foil. Use a knife to loosen the edges of the cake. Transfer it onto a wire rack and let it cool for about half an hour. Cover the pan once it's cool and store it in a fridge overnight.

• Remove it from the pan and serve with raspberries on top if you want.

Nutrition Information
• Calories: 187 calories
• Total Carbohydrate: 17 g
• Cholesterol: 46 mg
• Total Fat: 8 g
• Fiber: 1 g
• Protein: 8 g
• Sodium: 378 mg

www.ingramcontent.com/pod-product-compliance
Lightning Source LLC
Chambersburg PA
CBHW071445070526
44578CB00001B/210